*Communications
Canada
2000*

YORK UNIVERSITY

THE GERSTEIN LECTURE SERIES

Communications Canada 2000

PIERRE JUNEAU
GORDON B. THOMPSON
H. MARSHALL McLUHAN
DAVIDSON DUNTON

York University / Toronto

Canadian Cataloguing in Publication Data

Main entry under title:

Communications Canada 2000

(The Gerstein lectures ; 1975)

ISBN 0-919604-34-X bd. ISBN 0-919604-36-6 pa.

1. Mass media — Canada — Addresses, essays, lectures.   2. Mass media — Social aspects — Canada — Addresses, essays, lectures.   I. Juneau, Pierre, 1922 -   II. Series: The Frank Gerstein lectures ; 1975.

P92.C3C64   301.16'1'0971   C77-001292-2

The Gerstein Lectures,
York University,
4700 Keele Street,
Downsview, Ontario
M3J 1P3

Photocomposition of titles and text, in *Baskerville,* and assembly of reproduction prints by Publications Office, York University. Cover design by Michael Ecob. Printed in Canada by University of Toronto Press.

Foreword

These papers were presented on the occasion of the thirteenth Gerstein Lecture Series on March 6, 1975. The theme, *Communications Canada 2000,* is in line with the general structure of the Series, which is primarily designed to examine social phenomena in their relation to the university. The presentations here recorded aroused considerable interest and enthusiasm in their varied and comprehensive treatment of the subject of communications, and it is my belief that the ideas developed by these scholars will prove a stimulant in the fascinating study of communications today and tomorrow.

I would like to express my appreciation to the Frank Gerstein Charitable Foundation, which makes possible this annual Series; to Dean Joseph G. Green, who chaired and directed the 1974-75 Gerstein Lecture Committee; and particularly to the four lecturers who shared their ideas and expertise with us.

H. Ian Macdonald
President
York University

Contents

Introduction

JOSEPH G. GREEN

Many new Canadians are struck particularly by the rather constant stress on the importance of the communications media to this nation. The C.B.C. and its sister networks, we are told, have replaced the railroads as the vital system which can tie this diverse and dispersed nation together.

As firm believers in the responsibility of the contemporary university to confront issues of public policy and to serve as a forum for the articulation of views and visions about the future of our nation and the world, we of the Gerstein Lecture Committee found a lecture series on the role of communications in Canada in the year 2000 to be a natural and timely topic.

The four addresses gathered here were delivered to an audience of some four hundred students, teachers, and communications experts on a single day, March 6, 1975. Separately, each is a probing and personal statement about the future of Canada and the world. Taken together, they constitute a wide-ranging and deeply committed examination of the future role of the mass media.

The concerns raised by the speakers are shared by many who must come to grips with a world made ever more immediate by mass communications processes. From computer to citizens band radio, from cable television to laser technology, we are drawn inexorably toward the moment of instant interrelationships, toward a world where values tend to blur and the trivial grows to the size of the momentous, toward a path of continuous and constant sharing with an accompanying decrease in personal privacy and solitude.

The essays which follow, while they lack the immediacy of delivery by their speakers (this publication should really have been via video-disc), can place our concerns into a humane scale — a perspective with which we can deal — a proportion with which we can still feel comfortable as we peer into the murky clouds of the future.

Joseph G. Green, Dean
Faculty of Fine Arts
York University

Less Than Six Thousand Working Days to the Year 2000

PIERRE JUNEAU

Less Than Six Thousand Working Days to the Year 2000

PIERRE JUNEAU

Perhaps the most amazing feature of January 1, 2000 —
the first day of the new century — will be that nothing
earth-shattering is likely to occur on that day, nothing that
has not already started to affect the Western world. Events
will continue to bear out the same mixture of approximate
prediction and false prophecy. We must accept our inability
to predict adequately what the end of the century will be
like; too many contradictions, ruptures, and major
reorientations are waiting for us.

This is not, of course, sufficient reason to accept
increasing uncertainty and disorientation. In this sense, we
are living with enough contradictions right now. In fact, the
central contradictions and problems which will shape the
next quarter-century in the communications sector are
already all too visible. They are here now to discuss, to
analyze, perhaps even to solve.

However, they are not talked about very much, not even
by those with both the imagination and the responsibility to
tackle them. We have been dragging our feet in the task of
understanding media set for us by Marshall McLuhan a
decade ago. This is, I think, largely because we have been
too easily distracted by sub-issues, sub-effects, minor
accidents, and the wonder of technology in the field of
broadcasting and communication. We focus on the

proclivities of media content, such as violence and obscenity, almost to the exclusion of consideration of their general causes. Some people even seem to have stopped considering the whole system of causes and constraints, and focus their indignation on a subliminal picture that lasts only a twelfth of a second, ignoring the more basic fact that our total system of communication is subliminal.

As always, the most significant realities are least obvious. And if they are perceptible, we do not take time to agree even on the definitions and concepts with which to discuss them. In any case, they are rarely the subject of extensive public debate. The Surgeon-General of the United States can spend two million dollars amassing a two-foot shelf of reports on just one possible effect of media, that of violence, and not raise questions as to the economic and technological factors which lead to that effect.

Twenty-four years after the appearance of McLuhan's *Mechanical Bride,* we are still groping our way like sleep-walkers through a forest of systems and programs. We have yet to recognize that hidden but obstinate technological phenomena have a more durable effect on men than the minor episodes and accidents which preoccupy so much of our attention and effort. Perhaps if we are not up to making historic decisions daily, we can at least try to unveil some of the historic trends which will yield continuing influence on the technical and human organization of our means of communication.

Our communication technology has already reached an amazing degree of flexibility and adaptability. Yet we are still more fascinated by tinkering with the technology than by its purpose. Today, converging, compatible, inter-changeable systems of communication are replacing distinct communication sectors. These new systems are capable of combining any message with any means of processing or delivery. The same film, be it produced optically or on celluloid or coded on magnetized oxide on plastic tape, can be transmitted by Hertzian waves through space; can share a microwave facility or a satellite with computer data or telephone conversations on their way to our homes; or can be transported around the city on a coaxial cable with twenty other lanes of information and entertainment. The same news source, the reporter and his typewriter, feeds the printed press, delivered by paper boy, and the wire service for other newspapers. This serves as copy for broadcast reading and ultimately is used as direct alphanumeric information electronically printed on our home screens. The telephone wire can just as easily transmit a family conversation, a letter, a photograph, or digital information for a computer.

Fundamental dimensions of social and cultural communications will have a deep effect on our social and moral crises. In a recent interview given to the French magazine *Réalités,* Marshall McLuhan even went so far as to predict doom if the world does not get rid of television. For many, the processes of imaginative invention and creative development are taken for granted, but technical possibilities seem social necessities. Once these necessities are taken care of — these technical, financial, industrial, engineering necessities — it is assumed that creative production will just happen. It is like traffic on telephone lines: you set up the lines, but you do not have to worry about their use. People will just talk. Indeed, that is perhaps why we get so much talk on radio and television. The problem is, however, that *creative* production would require as much research, planning, and development of systems and economic policies, as much application of intelligence and imagination, as technological works.

The industrial and the technological logic and relativism that preside over the development of communication tools also predetermine the content of the system. As a result one can confidently predict further systematic overthrow of norms, social inhibitions, and aesthetic constraints, making really banal the kind of media aggression we used to know. Perhaps we are caught in a Darwinian struggle between families of tools and techniques on the one hand and their functions on the other. We should not be astonished by the rapid succession of moral, social, economic, and political crises if we support and plan only the development of tools which accelerate these crises.

One can argue that the real revolution will continue to be a cultural revolution, and that some of the more difficult economic problems such as inflation and consumption already have strong cultural implications. Certainly their relationship to communication is obvious if one only thinks about how broadcasting is financed, and how program policies are determined.

Closed off as we are in a technological universe, more automated than we realize, it is going to take more than a renewal of merchandising strategy, more than new appeals for self-restraint, to assure continued growth of our civilization. It is precisely because we have shut ourselves off in this scientific, technological universe that rhetorical, philosophic, legislative, literary, even theological innovations are needed. These may become the central disciplines to reinforce if we are to expect any new possibilities of leadership, credibility, or orientation. These are perhaps the disciplines that can throw new light on what is rapidly becoming a central problem — that of the man-machine relationship.

We are promised home computer terminals by the end of the century. Our television sets can already offer a choice of twenty channels. Wall-screen TV projectors are being marketed now in the United States; there are some in Canada in taverns and pubs.

In this new culture of push-buttons and cathode tubes

and electronic pipes, the very forms and values of our work
and leisure are being modified. This man-machine interface
forces on us a fundamental reconsideration of craft, of art,
of cultural production, in fact of all forms of human
creations and expressions. The powerful maturing and
voracious systems of hardware can only make software
problems more acute — problems of production policy;
problems of discovery, promotion, and encouragement of
human talent; problems of programming strategy;
problems of cultural anxiety; even problems of cultural
fatigue. These problems are not abstract; it is simply a fact
that the rapid technical advance in carrying and processing
images and data in the last fifteen years has not been
matched in any way by a parallel or adequate improvement
in the quality and the quantity of software or content.

The Canadian Radio and Television Commission has
been stressing this point for several years. I have even
characterized the hardware obsession, in an expression that
is obviously excessive, as a "technological cancer". The
hardware-software imbalance was the most obvious concern
at the CBC hearing held in the spring of 1974. Software
problems will become a much-debated subject in board
rooms and public forums, whether the focus is on more
inventive programs for huge computers, the renewal of
television series, the marketing of video discs, the
production of educational, informational, or entertainment
programs, image invention, or even moral or ethical
expression. One can easily predict that the symptoms of the
illness of our systems — problems such as vulgarity,
cynicism, violence, and commercialist distortions — will
continue to occupy attention and cause irritation.

And no doubt the frustration and irritation will grow as
we experience the inability to rid the patient of the symptoms. The present logic or method of communication has in-
differently eroded the human imagination, has eliminated

or obscured classical forms and models, has held nearly
every value up to ridicule, has even made it almost impossible to think of generous or integrating images or symbols
or, to borrow Marshall McLuhan's terminology, the patterns
the artist produces to get us out of the maelstrom.

We still have barely scratched the surface in studying the
strange relationship between art and technology, that logic
of the circulation of cultural products which controls the
evolution of moral and aesthetic norms. We endlessly
discuss the taste, the crimes, the immorality of the media
when we should be paying equal attention to the dimensions
of program series, the proportion of rerun material, the
problem of supply, strategy of networks, structure of
investments, the extent of neglected or even ignored human
creative resources. We face an industrialization of the
imagination — a revolution every bit as fundamental as the
mechanization of industry and the labour force.

The price we have paid for a zealous marketplace concept
of broadcasting has been systematic automation, stretching,
reuse, even brutalization of the fragile human talent and
inventiveness which is supposed to provide the thousands of
hours of content the system requires. When this system is in
full free operation, the result should not be surprising. Can
you imagine the schizophrenia of network managers who
have to plan and schedule thirty-four hundred hours of
programming every year, including at least five hundred
hours of really expensive production? Who have to somehow
keep the huge audience fascinated? Who are beset by
problems of program supply at the right price? And who
know that the system will have to be carried by more cheap
programs or reruns than may be conscionable?

In this efficient if paradoxical world, mechanization of
scripts means the endless repetition of the same plot
elements: violence disguised as a dramatic resolution,
myriad settings for the same single idea, a sort of

well-packaged predictability masquerading as "what the people want". If Charlie Chaplin were to remake *Modern Times* today, perhaps instead of satirizing the assembly lines of the thirties, he would focus on the absurdities and tragedies of the mechanization of drama or variety, even of the rawest of all resources for the media, the talking head.

Remedies will not be easy. Industrial and technological logic, whether it be in the field of automobiles, television, or photography, tends all too easily to favour quantifiable concepts at the expense of the less tangible qualitative aspects. In that sense, it is true the medium is still the message, if one is referring to the way in which the systems modify mental and even physical landscapes. But the complexity of our system of information makes it necessary to resist the somewhat fatal domination or neglect of the message by the medium.

Let me refer again to the subject of violence, which I have described as a symptom of a more fundamental problem. There is more and more talk about it both in Canada and in the United States. But the managers of the most important production lines in television, the programming heads of the three American networks, develop more series that include violence. The North American system was designed that way. American TV represents the least constrained form of marketplace mass medium and so must rely heavily on a mechanized approach to the dramatic and the fictional.

At the beginning of the 1974-75 television season, there were twenty-three action-adventure police-detective stories on U.S. networks in prime time. More than half of the January second season, as it is called, were of the same genre. To the managers of program development and production who must play within the rules of the game, it is the form of television most likely to achieve commercial success.

To a limited extent each country can decide what the rules will be. As yet, no other country in the world, Canada included, has this problem as an internal phenomenon to quite the same extent. In an analysis of over fifty programs, nearly equally divided between U.S. and Canadian, during times of heavy viewing by children, ninety-five percent of all violent acts occurred in U.S.-made shows. However, if we let that system completely dominate our own approach to television, the figures would quickly change. And, of course, let's not be too righteous about it; we already import a large proportion of the most violent U.S. shows.

Let's look closely at the industrial-mechanized market approach to broadcasting from another point of view. Recently we compared the prime-time television schedules from Canada, the United States, the United Kingdom, and Germany. To simplify this analysis, colours were given to the major types of television programming. All drama shows, from situation comedy to police-action-adventure, were shaded orange. Variety and game shows were green, and news, current affairs, and documentaries were blue. The Canadian schedule, while dominated by the orange, still had a flow of blues and greens on both CBC and CTV. The British and German schedules were colourful mosaics, their networks blending colours with the passing of each half hour. However, the American schedule was something quite different, with only three hours on the commercial networks indicating a colour other than orange.

In effect, the production line dictated the competitive homogeneity of programming across the schedules, a production line set up to serve a mass-market philosophy, as compared to those designed to serve a public purpose. The demands of that technology and structure were indeed dictating the shape of the messages, the contents which were transmitted over the public airways. The different philosophy of the British, German, and, to a certain extent, Canadian networks indicates that the message can, at times, overcome the medium.

This can further be seen in the range of children's television programming found on Canadian and British television when compared to the products of the production line. In the U.S. the product is almost exclusively cartoons, and these cartoons are ingrained with the same types of violent conflict found in evening programming. Again, the plant has dictated the message.

It seems invidious to refer repeatedly to "the U.S." as compared to "Canada". We are not comparing the two countries, but rather the slightly different technological and industrial and marketing systems which produce the different situations in the two countries.

In Canada, twenty years of domestic production for children in the public sector has produced programming which is notably free of violence, offering a rather convincing proof that if we understand the purposes of the medium rather than be swayed by its constraint, if we remember the intent of the messages we are setting out to convey, we can enhance the software element in our system of broadcasting.

When the public interest is placed above strictly marketplace considerations, diversity and imagination can flourish. The evidence is clear: the CBC's children's programming, CTV on Saturday mornings, TVA in Quebec or Ontario's OECA. British and European television reflect a similar orientation, as does the public service-oriented Children's Television Workshop in the U.S.

The real contradiction in our broadcasting and communication systems today arises from a slavish mouthing of clichés inappropriate to gatherings of men and women with considerable public responsibility for enormous cultural problems which blatantly affect both our economic and political fate. This is a very serious reason for changing our attitudes today in order to build a more viable system over the next twenty-five years. Let's step behind the software and the programming problems for a moment and consider briefly how the user, the communication consumer, is being treated. We are told that broadcasting by its nature is based on a mass-market economy and must reap the largest number of people either to survive economically in the private sector or, as was once argued in the case of the public sector, to justify the taxpayers' dollars. This argument, though heard so often, is flabbier than it sounds. We subsidize higher education that benefits only a tiny percentage of the population because we have been convinced that its spin-off effect in the whole society warrants such a concentration of effort. Is it so difficult to justify high quality, enlightening broadcasts that might reach less than a marketable audience?

And let's analyze more rigorously the so-called "mass audience" that is vied for and catered to so assiduously.

It is a little discussed fact that only one-fifth of the population accounts for just about one-half of all the viewing done and two-fifths of the whole population accounts for seventy percent of all the viewing done. If we analyze the consequences of this fact, we might question the habit of talking about the success of broadcasting only in terms of the "mass" who are watching or listening. Are not these heavy viewers really a minority themselves, in terms of the spectrum of the whole society with its range of ages, backgrounds, interests, and even in terms of what this other four-fifths buys and consumes?

The medium may be loaded, of course, with traditional constraints, but these must not prevent an adequate, reasonable discussion of a quality of life and a balance of culture that is dominated neither by the inherent tendency of the technology to industrially strip-mine the most ready resources nor by the economy of Madison Avenue. Is it forbidden to at least think of a truly modern, egalitarian society and culture in which we are free to choose among all forms of expression, freely exposed to a real variety of information on which to make public choices? Is it forbidden to think of using the modern electronic media to offset mass concepts, mass behaviour, mass reactions, mass manipulation, and mass psychology? I fully realize that in making such a statement and even in suggesting goals of diversity and selectivity for our system of communication, I am raising all too obviously what some people consider the ugly ogre of audience fragmentation. I know with what dread this particular concept is held. After all, it describes what happens when more channels or stations arrive in an area and the same audience is divided into smaller units. But is not the concept almost meaningless under the terms set out by a twenty, thirty, or forty channel technology itself? More important, doesn't an audience that is truly fragmented reflect what we all know: namely, that most people don't like being lumped together in a single pot? Perhaps the more truly fragmented and diverse the audience for different types of entertainment and information, the more successful we would be in a larger sense. Of course, if the fragmentation is mainly the result of reshuffling the same material, then the system becomes self-destructive, competing with itself, like a serpent eating its tail or like a percolator which does not replace the coffee but recirculates water over and over again through the same coffee.

Looking at this question positively, there is even a hope that diverse, fragmented audiences might have some value for the range of advertisers who at present have to take a barrelful of ages, sexes, income groups, and interests to reach the particular section of the population that is interested in their particular product. The use of multiple channels and diverse programming aimed at targeted audience groups should interest these specialized advertisers. This may sound like a broadcasting fantasy — but it is worth far more consideration, far more serious research effort, especially at the level of audience measurement tools and techniques, than is presently being undertaken.

We now have in place the mechanisms of promoting this diversity but, as we have seen demonstrated, the choice has yet to arrive on our screens. Brian De Palma, a talented film director, has noted that industrialization of programming for television has resulted in a situation where TV has used up all the plots. Viewers know it all by heart. You just cannot do the old genres any more. Another director cannot do the old Alfred Hitchcock formula any more than Hitchcock can. Yet at the same time, we have created systems which place an unprecedented demand on new creativity and innovation. And it is this talent that ends up at the very bottom of the economic heap in broadcasting and perhaps in communications generally. If software is to take centre stage, the authors and performers cannot be far behind. It may be painful to state the obvious but no camera is lined up, no studio lit, no control room manned, no set built, no advertising hits the street, until writers deliver the scripts and performers get up to perform. Yet today in this country the average salary for a member of the Association of Canadian Television and Radio Artists is below that of a secretary. Film-makers drive taxi cabs. Opera singers work in liquor stores. Musicians stay home and have babies. Writers become public relations men. Dancers wait on tables. Animated film producers go bankrupt. I am referring to one of the best animators in this country, Jerry Potterton, whose company went bankrupt some time ago, and I could put names behind all those examples. Even our more important authors must write petitions to be assured of a livelihood.

Naturally, many talented Canadians are making livings comparable to those that can be garnered in more established careers. But it is a cruel marketplace that

overexposes one personality every evening for several years
or encourages only one group of known celebrities. In a
recessional economic period, it may be unpopular to talk of
creating employment opportunities for jugglers or folk-
singers, but it is not a charity at all. As pointed out before,
in a broadcasting system which has almost a half-billion
dollars to spend annually, only three million dollars end up
in the pockets of writers. I often marvel at the perseverance
and the drive that keeps performers in this country doing
what they are doing, and also at the fact that television
commercials are often more lucrative to actors and actresses
than domestic television drama. Consider the efficiencies of
television as a medium of expression: a CBC television
production of the Theatre Passe Muraille can be seen by
more people in a single hour than is possible in an entire
year of performance on their small Toronto stage; a Sunday
afternoon concert by a string quartet will be heard and seen
by more people than could fill the National Arts Centre
theatre each night for that same year. Providing national
audiences of a quarter of a million people for so-called
minority forms of entertainment is more than a charitable
service for the performers.

It is a strange society that gladly accepts an architect's five
to ten percent commission on the total cost of a building and
yet considers the author and writer worth only about one
percent of the industry that relies so heavily on his or her
skills. We complain every day about the lack of variety and
good design in our cityscapes. We seldom worry about the
same lack of surprise and stimulation in our media
environment and even less look for the cause.

The inadequacy of our cultural economy can be illustrat-
ed in a great many ways. So can the manner of our technological enthusiasm outweigh our cultural intelligence. To
take another well-known example, we all know that we are
in an era of generalized copying and re-recording of

the intellectual and creative works of the few. It may be just a matter of time until more blank cassettes are sold than records, until more blank paper is used for photocopying than for the entire output of publishing, until visual piracy will be undertaken institutionally as well as privately, as a simple matter of course. Libraries in the United States are right now being accused of such systematic dissemination of copies from journals that the practice has been called "a colossal unauthorized use of the intellectual property upon which the whole system rests."

So we should rethink the entire structure and economics of cultural productions and communications now. If at the beginning of these six thousand days we undertake this with imagination, intelligence, and determination, we may reach the year 2000 in a better state of mind and body.

In this kind of perspective, the future of a civilization which was built on the controlled circulation of works of the imagination or the intellect may be in jeopardy indeed.

It must be clear, then, why public bodies can hardly avoid being involved in a successful scenario for the coming decades. A fundamental economic re-evaluation is needed. Certainly, the artist and creator cannot himself escape the realities of today's technical and economic organization. That is not to say that the performing arts, film, the theatre, or even independent television production have become heavy industries. On the contrary. However, artistic creation must find a positive relation to the realities of mass diffusion. The most lonely craftsman or painter cannot survive today without some access to, and therefore effect on, promotion and distribution systems.

This change has come about because of the expanding role of new families of tools which now seem indispensible. Goya or Varley needed no outside encouragement to start drawing. Artists could starve to death and still keep working. But artistic expression, just like information, is increasingly tied to the operation of complex and competitive technologies such as satellite switching systems and expensive and efficient production, recording, and copying machines. Indeed, it is more likely that it is the arts collectively which will die more quickly than the individual artist. Even sports, supported by an enthusiastic public, flourish only to the degree that they meet the needs of huge media systems. Consider the massive Olympic enterprise: that is what the future will be like if we do not encourage other principles of production and programming based on diversification rather than on world concentration of attention and financial resources.

When the future tools of world success and simultaneity, such as the direct home satellite, begin to operate, there will certainly be a role for the state as a mediator in the difficult relationship which will exist among the media giants and between these powerful agents and other legitimate, smaller-scale users of the system. Such conditions represent the price we must pay when nearly every form of communication and expression is served by massive financial, industrial, and technological structures.

The arts and journalism are already up against the wall of technological, economic, and administrative problems. In a way both the media businessmen and the lone creator are caught in the same dilemma. The creator cannot ignore the industrial dimension of his work and the entrepreneur cannot for long ignore the source of supply in a demanding media technology — unless we follow Marshall McLuhan's suggestion and get rid of the whole thing. Maybe that is what the public will do at some point.

The marketplace context is already developed and will become further entrenched in the decades ahead, and only the largest multinational entertainment enterprises are likely to be able to prosper without the benefit of public policy framework. We are facing, I think, an inexorable increase in the number and power of executive and supervisory bodies in the field of the arts — that same field once characterized by lonely and solitary efforts.

The result? Great promise or great threat, depending largely on the qualities of knowledgeable public debate which animate these activities and depending also on a willingness to curb the ritual confrontation between creators and businessmen, policy makers and policy consumers. It is not enough for a government to learn to speak the language of the arts and of the public. Each citizen and each creator must also learn to consider the collective concerns of the public service. If the state is to provide policies which foster the necessary human qualities of imagination and harmony, we had better lay to rest one myth right away: the myth that any government intervention in the arts is a form of protection and interference which almost inevitably leads to mediocrity. This is an incredibly erroneous interpretation of the well-known history of cultural development in the world. It must be acknowledged that the competitive marketplace has produced some remarkable results, of which the American pre-war cinema is perhaps the best example. However, most of the best works of great art — painting, architecture, music, ballet, opera, theatre, and more recently even cinema and television — are the result of either direct or indirect public action through the state. The so-called free marketplace tends to reinforce the strongest, resulting in the rigid organization of the celebrity and star market.

The responsibility of the public authority is to correct imbalances in the economic framework so that the weaker can survive as well as the strong. And the weaker economically is not always the weaker in terms of talent and creativity. In the field of ideas and creativity it is the fostering of the framework in which not only the great industrial powers of production, information, entertainment, and knowledge can mass-produce and mass-distribute their products for the largest common denominator, but also allowing those who do not belong to the largest common denominator to have some choice and opportunity of their own.

Such an idea presupposes a public commitment to restructure the economic framework in which the entrepreneur and the creator must work together. It presupposes a concerted approach to identify and promote not only talent but also critical, analytical, and managerial skills in the fields of cultural production and circulation. And a prerequisite is the need to position artistic and expressive activities accurately in the social and economic structure of society.

For over a century now, men have explored the economic and social implications of industrialization. We have found it beneficial to encourage industry through tax policies, depreciation allowances, and other measures, all leading to a stimulation of our society through industrial expansion. Today we are beginning to question the policies of exponential growth with its accompanying planned obsolescence. The high price we are paying now for energy supplies reminds us that perhaps we have too many automobiles and not enough children's theatre companies or orchestras. The endless re-inventing of different brand names of instant coffee seems to have replaced the literary battles of the nineteenth century.

Other countries have re-evaluated their concepts of the economics of work. They consider not just the value of goods but the value added to those goods by intensive industrial processes. We must also realize that value-added concepts may be even more appropriate for the creation of artistic goods — an intensive field of human activity if there ever was one. A Canada Council study has shown that every penny of subsidy to the performing arts circulates through the economy and contributes to the prosperity of many other diverse activities.

We must understand the need to recognize the contribution that artists and artisans can still make, even in economic terms, in a world of instant electronic transmissions and manned space capsules. And let us remember that a mile of urban expressway costs twenty million dollars. I would suggest, too, that a more integrated planning approach in the field of culture is the only one that can possibly succeed. Can we really discuss public goals for television and think that somehow the film industry is located on a distant planet? Or can we answer the needs of film-makers, and shuffle writers to some other department on the pretext that they work only with words and reference documents? There is always the tendency in complex, mechanized societies to treat this intangible sector as some form of peripheral subsistence activity.

In this last quarter of this twentieth century, we will not be able to ignore the fundamental importance of re-establishing the balance in priorities between the tools of communication and the purpose of communication.

It is said of Henry David Thoreau that when people announced to him, with some amazement, that a first conversation had taken place at a distance over a piece of wire (later called the telephone), his only response was: "Oh, what did they say?"

But allow me to conclude on a note of typical television viewer candor and optimisim. After eight years of police investigation, the Canadian actor Raymond Burr decided to get out of his wheelchair, drop his role as Chief Robert Ironside, undergo a slight metamorphosis and re-emerge as a doctor. Inspired by such a symbolic vision, one can only wonder at the perspective of healing and comfort this transformation will open up for our collective souls and bodies.

Technical and Research Aspects of Communication

GORDON B. THOMPSON

Technical and Research Aspects of Communication

GORDON B. THOMPSON

Life in the year 2000 cannot be a simple extrapolation of the consumption-oriented genre we knew in the past. Let us therefore have done with the communications innovations that, like the comet Kohoutek, are all froth and no substance. To have any meaning in terms of the difficulties that face our society, the contributions from communications will have to be more fundamental than anything we have seen lately.

Many of the much talked about communications innovations are mere system component improvements with little or no power to transform the communication medium to which they are applied. Have satellites, lasers, or fibre optics changed things in any significant way? No! They are merely improvements made in some larger system that was already in place, where the potential for qualitative change has been achieved already.

It seems almost as if Alchemy rather than Science has been the foundation of the basic decisions made, both here and in other countries, about communications innovations over the past few decades. Once made, however, these decisions have triggered some really good scientific effort. Consider, for example, the video telephone. Although some very outstanding scientific work was done in achieving the service objectives, anything but good scientific methodology was used in determining what those objectives should have been. The development of the silicon target vidicon camera tube, which was sufficiently robust to withstand looking at the sun, illustrates the technical achievements made to bring this service into being. On the other hand, no body of scientific literature exists that establishes the proper nature of such a service, its usefulness, or its utility.

Canada, being at least among the leaders if not *the* leader in communications technology deployment, will have few opportunities to dumbly follow the lead of other countries. The knowledge and research needed in the future will not be so much in the classical areas of hardware problems, but rather in generating insights into how that hardware ought to be used.

My own research during the past half decade has been directed toward assessment of communications innovations, in terms that are quite removed from the immediate financial costs and rewards. There has never been any shortage of ideas in the communications industry, only a problem of which idea to choose and which to reject. This problem is particularly acute because of the long time intervals involved between decision making and actual service introduction in the capital intensive world of telecommunications. It is not design aids we need, but rather decision making aids. For this reason, it was decided to stress the idea of assessment rather than design.

In launching this work, our operating hypothesis was that if one did something that produced in our society the same kinds of impacts that the previous great communications revolutions produced in their societies, then what was done would also be seen as a communications revolution. The measure of significance of the past communications revolutions must surely lie in the impacts these innovations had on their host societies, so an analysis was made of relevant literature, and a conceptual basis for an assessment methodology was developed. Because recent wounds so limit our perceptions, modern innovations were set aside, and particular attention was paid to older, well established innovations.

If the literature on successful past communications innovations is fuzzy, then the literature on the failure of communications innovations is non-existent. We had to turn to modern blunders to develop the constraints needed for assessment. Our conceptual base was therefore developed from ancient successes and recent disappointments. Some attempt was made to locate and analyze older failures from the skimpy records that still do exist, Ontario's colonization roads being a case in point, and these efforts produced results that corroborated the findings from the more recent data.

This process, to date, has produced three characterizations of communications revolutions, together with two constraints, all based on the effects produced by past communications revolutions on their host societies. From here, it was a short step to build an admittedly simplistic measuring instrument which system designers and decision makers could use along with their more conventional but less creative tools.

The First Characterization: Access to Stored Experience

Each communications revolution made stored human experience easier to access. This ease was manifested by an increased use of stored human experience in the daily transactions of men. Here we have two notions: stored human experience was always made easier to access, and there was more accessing done.

The adoption of the phonetic alphabet by the Greeks, between the ninth and fifth centuries B.C., is a fine example of how a significant change in the ease of accessing stored human experience can affect a whole society. Writing had existed before the phonetic alphabet, but was very clumsy and good only for such purposes as the making of lists and bookkeeping. These early forms of writing required much effort to learn and maintain. By adding vowels to the Phoenician consonants, the Greeks completed the elements required to produce a pronounceable writing form. This simple adaptation resulted in a skill that could be taught in just a few years and was easy to maintain. So the number of users multiplied rapidly.

Even the telephone makes stored human experience easier to access. It is so easy to find out something through the use of the telephone that we frequently overlook its importance in this area. Much of the efficiency of today's world of commerce depends on this aspect of the telephone.

Although the computer has made a considerable contribution toward easing the access to stored human experience, it has been somewhat disappointing in view of the promise many of the experts saw a decade or so ago. Linguistic research has identified what may be a fundamental constraint limiting the utility of information retrieval systems, language translation systems and the like. Yehoshua Bar-Hillel presents the argument that really effective general purpose information systems are impossible to build; yet we cannot afford to stop trying.

It seems that ordinary language is too varied and complex in its structure to be analyzed adequately by mere Aristotelian logic. In linguistically simplified situations — those employing formal or technical vocabularies, for example, and particularly in mission oriented environments — machine retrieval systems can function superbly.

Our many, fine, specialized, computer information retrieval systems are really quite limited in their application, and Bar-Hillel cautions us against over-generalizing from our particular successes. He cautions us on the one hand, but expresses a fond desire on the other that his pessimism may be proven unnecessary. He proves the impossibility of fully automatic machine processing of common, generally used, language, while almost in the same breath suggesting that we cannot afford to stop trying! Such is the essence of a conundrum. In recognition of Bar-Hillel's far-sightedness in seeing these difficulties while everyone else was singing the opposite tune, we have chosen to name this linguistic constraint "Bar-Hillel's conundrum". This constraint limits aspects of all three characterizations of communications revolutions.

The really significant achievements in easing the access to stored human experience have had the effect of modifying or changing the way people indexed information. The printing press, for example, caused references to change from the Biblical New Testament form of "it is written" to citation of the exact volume in which the writing could be found. The computer spawned new indexing systems, such as the "Key Word in Context" system. A test for significance under this first characterization can be made by asking if a particular communications innovation has the potential of affecting how people index information.

The Second Characterization: Common Information Space

People operate in many spaces beyond the merely physical one. There is the concept of an activity space, such as a person's job or role. There are also information spaces that people occupy and identify with.

Conversation represents a rather interesting manifestation of a spatial game played in an information space. The acoustic space enveloping two conversants is occupied, at first glance, by one person and then the other, alternately; and a well understood game is played when one wishes to retire or the other wishes to advance into possession of that space. The really exciting moments occur during interruptions, when both communicants try to occupy that space simultaneously. It is perhaps during these brief moments that the major emotional catharsis occurs.

The familiar model in which communicants alternate their possession of the information space ignores the importance of those moments of dual occupancy.

A common or mutually shared information space must exist for communication to occur. For example, we must speak the same language; our use of special terms must stem from common experience; we must be where we can hear each other. The efficiency, effectiveness, depth, and involvement of the communication experience all seem to vary directly with the size of the common information space shared by the communicants.

Widely available books permit an increase in the size of the information space people can share. By reading the same book, many can share a common information space, because the copies they read are identical. This permits subsequent exchanges between them to be richer, for they now have more grist for their conversation.

Every significant communications development seems to have increased the size of the common information space the communicants could share. This is the second characterization of communications revolutions.

We communicate using many languages, both verbal and non-verbal. The more of these we can share simultaneously in any communications situation, the richer the experience can be. Interruptions of one language can be achieved by means of another, as when gesture interrupts a speaker. The larger the size of the shared information space, the richer the choice of interrupt strategies becomes. The game becomes more involving, interactive, and exciting.

The range of interrupt strategies open to the communicants provides a significance test for this characterization. It is not necessary that the communicants actually use the whole range of interrupt strategies; they need only be aware of the extent of that range. Conflict resolution studies show that the unsent message is almost as valuable as the sent message, so long as both parties know the channel is open.

The "I-see-you, you-see-me" videophone kind of service does not create a shared visual space, for I am looking at you while you are looking at me. A simple game of naughts and crosses cannot be played with ease on such a system. Your naughts are on the screen in front of my face, while my crosses are on a sheet of paper on my table. There is no display that shows both the naughts and the crosses together, except as a player creates one by copying what is seen on his screen onto the paper in front of him.

However, such a service concept does represent a small increase over the telephone in terms of the size of the common information space shared by the communicants. The basis for this increase is the increase in the range of interrupt strategies, for gestures can be used for interrupts. However, the deletion of the handset, which is replaced by a switched audio channel, permitting a "hands-free" style of use, represents a lessening of the acoustic shared information space, so the whole effect may be little changed from the much simpler telephone.

In the early days of the mail, a letter could change the whole path of the recipient's life. It provided the potential for an interrupt that was not widely available before the Penny Post service began.

A computer based management system where each person's files are kept in a central storage system has been built. Browse routines make it easy to peruse each other's work. Clearly such a system enlarges the size of the information space shared by the system users. Interrupts would be of the form, "Say, I see you are thinking about widgets. Did you know that Professor I.M. Wong in Saskatoon has done quite a lot with widgets?"

Unfortunately, such an enlargement appears constrained, in the limit, by Bar-Hillel's conundrum. The problem is the browse routines. Improvements in the intellectual side of this shared information space characterization appear to have an upper bound.

The Third Characterization: Nascent Consensus

The third characterization of communications revolutions relates to the ease with which new ideas can be propagated throughout the society. Each significant communications revolution has increased the ease with which shared feelings could be discovered and developed in the host society. For want of a better name, I choose to call this process the development and discovery of nascent consensus. We are not concerned with beating the remaining twenty-five percent of the population into submission, but rather with how the first ten percent got the thing going in the first place.

Money is one of the greatest consensus producing social inventions man has produced. In a very simple, direct, and positive way it determines how many Mustangs will be built, how much bread will be baked, and how many bridges will be constructed.

The choosing of popular songs is another example of a consensus forming system. This system is based on record sales and various other techniques that indicate the preferences of listeners to radio and television. It is a complex, fast acting system. As our communications environment evolved from the concert hall to include radio and television, the musical consensus system speeded up and became more pluralistic and complex. It also became easier to input the system with new musical ideas.

B.F. Skinner has observed that the significant characterization of evolution relates to increases of a being's, or
culture's, sensitivity to the remote consequences of its
actions. Perhaps his observation is less global if we note that
mass media that absorb too much information, and hence
attenuate too much variety, have an inherent propensity to
produce just this result. We have gone through a period of
intense development of such media over the last century.

The development of widely used, consensus spawning
communications systems that encourage the growth of
constructive and positive consensus seems both desirable
and difficult. We can do it where the messages are abstract,
as in the example of popular music, but where the messages
are explicit, as in politics, we seem quite unskilled. One
might be tempted to suggest that the power of the computer
could help here, but again Bar-Hillel's conundrum limits
such strategies.

An indication of the significance of advances under this
consensus characterization can be developed from the
probability of one's receiving messages that are both
exciting and unexpected. To the extent that this probability
can be enhanced, the formation of the intellectual
groupings that are the essence of consensus would be
enhanced as well.

The library scientist's concept of information profiles is
not a complete answer. Suppose that a researcher subscribes
to an information system that supplies him with abstracts
against his information profile. It is only logical that
abstracts of his own work would be included. This material
would not be unexpected. Any competent worker should
find the vast majority of messages selected through such a
process rather dull and quite predictable — just the
opposite of what we are looking for under this test. We are
seeking only those messages that are both unexpected and
exciting — quite a different thing. Shades of Maxwell's

demon. Bar-Hillel's conundrum limits our ability to solve this problem.

To this point, we have described three characterizations of communications that sprang from an analysis of the effects of communications revolutions on the societies in which these revolutions occurred. The three characterizations are:

- the ease with which stored human experience can be accessed,
- the size of the common information space shared by the communicants,
- the ease of discovery and development of nascent consensus.

And the three tests of significance which correspond to these characterizations are:

- must affect the way people index information,
- must increase the range of interrupt strategies open to the communicants for the interrupt act,
- must increase the probability of transmitting or receiving interesting but unexpected messages.

The three tests provide a basis for ordination which permits the development of useful instruments for the assessment of communication innovations. Let us now turn to the second constraint (the first constraint, Bar-Hillel's condundrum, having been dealt with as the three characterizations were being described).

The Second Constraint: Conviviality

The second constraint is an economic one, more complex than just the simple notion that the innovation must provide a payoff for the entrepreneur.

The effect of any really significant past communications revolution was to produce in the host society a significant increase in the ways ordinary citizens could earn money. The wealth creating processes of the society expanded so that more people participated in more ways. The "zero sum" economic game turned into an "everybody wins" game for a brief period of time. The important communications revolutions appear to have altered the environment in which the economic system was embedded, and so opened up whole new ways of creating wealth.

The economic effects of such a happening are truly profound. Conventional economic analysis can only lead to an entirely inadequate assessment of these opportunities. Rather than being merely limiting, this second constraint suggests the opportunity to develop new communications media to elicit the evolution of what one might call "convivial capitalism", to expand on Ivan Illich's terminology.

Illich uses the term "convivial tools" to describe tools and processes that have high utility for common folk. In his terms, the cooking stove and the hammer are very convivial tools, for almost everyone can use them to advantage. The computer, as we now know it, is anything but a convivial tool. By simplifying the chore of learning to read and write, the phonetic alphabet turned reading and writing into a highly convivial technology. Illich argues the essential importance of convivial tools to the stability and success of a society.

The telephone is a highly convivial communications tool, for anyone can use it reasonably well. Television is less convivial for, although we all can view it, only a few are sufficiently skilled to be able to input the TV medium well enough to make the result worth significant viewing time. Newspapers and other one-way mass media are similar in their level of conviviality. Such mass media must lie between the telephone and the post office at the high end of the conviviality scale, and the computer at the low end.

The major communications revolutions impacted their host society's economic environment by placing a new tool of increased conviviality in the society's hands, providing the opportunity for new wealth creating processes to emerge throughout that society. The printing press created the opportunity for the entrepreneurs of Europe to discover the publishing business. The previous technology, that of the Scriptorium, being so limited in throughput, was chiefly concerned with conservation. In this climate, there is little wonder why ancient works dominated that culture. Creativity and exploration are extremely costly if the price is possible loss of material that has been previously accumulated through very hard work. Here, then, is the link between easing the access to stored human experience and innovation, and, eventually, wealth creation.

Communications innovations that are high in conviviality and are also consensus builders appear to impinge directly upon the processes that are basic to the wealth creating means of a society. An examination of the various communications innovations of the past shows that consensus building and conviviality do not always occur together. Television is certainly a consensus building medium, but it is not a highly convivial one. However, the subset of the consensus systems that encourage the building of positive consensus, consensus that is forward directing rather than constraining, may well correlate with the set of communications innovations that are highly convivial.

The important thing the use of this communications innovation assessment technique teaches is that it is not the technology by itself that is dominant, but rather the manner in which that technology is coupled into the societal processes. The business arrangements, the content generation processes, the way in which the costs are allocated, are decisive factors in determining the role a communications medium plays in a society. This assessment technique is sensitive to these questions. It brings a fresh conceptual framework to the viewing of communications innovations. Consider, for example, the astronomer, as he peers through his telescope, viewing a distant star. If he fits his spectroscope on the telescope, he gets a totally different interpretation of that star. Both views are correct, in that they are each partial pictures of the whole. Similarly, the conventional, more mundane assessment methodologies used to probe communications innovations, and this particular assessment technique, both produce partial images of the whole story. Nor do they conflict, any more than the representational image of a star competes with its spectroscopic image.

Given this caveat, and the particular insights that this way of looking at communications innovations can generate, what can one see developing out of already existing technologies that could have major significance by the turn of the century? Two particular opportunities appear very interesting.

One of these areas of interest uses two new and emerging technical developments. It represents an amalgamation of computers, communications, and interactive intelligent graphics terminals structured so as to look good under this assessment technique. The other opportunity area is a variant of television, but again structured so as to obtain good marks under this particular method of assessing communications innovations.

Looking first at the computer based opportunity area, the first of the two technical developments is the trend in the prosaic telephone network toward digital transmission and switching. The very survival of existing service levels in the telephone network necessitates this conversion to the more efficient digital technique. This is an evolutionary change that began in the centre of the network, and is slowly working its way out to the edges. These changes produce real efficiencies in prosaic telephone service. It is rare good fortune when an innovation that was designed to satisfy efficiency objectives only turns out to have important radical significance. Digitization of the telephone network appears to be this kind of innovation.

The second technological development is the emergence of the intelligent peripheral. This is jargon for what happens to your telephone or your television set when integrated circuits become so cheap as to allow micro-computers to be incorporated in them. The recent history of the personal calculator should dispel any doubts about the reality of this possibility. Clearly, the inclusion of such intelligence would produce a communications device that is radically different from its antecedents.

The combination of these two emerging developments offers an opportunity to develop communications services that appear to have the potential of outranking the printing press for significance.

The intelligent interactive graphics terminal is a device that can show moving cartoons with less bandwidth than is required to transmit the human voice. It not only can show moving graphics, but also can be used to create such material. Like the telephone handset, it is both transmitter and receiver.

To put the concept of the intelligent interactive graphics terminal into context, let me recall that when I started at University, my slide rule cost seventeen dollars. My sons will pay about ten times that for a suitable calculator. Their children can probably expect to invest ten times that again for a word processing, graphics editing intelligent interactive terminal of their own. If present trends continue, that will also be the cost of a colour television set.

Because of the potential of such a terminal device, we have given it a more understandable name: "Scribblephone". At its simplest level, the Scribblephone concept provides a common graphic space that communicants can share, just as the telephone creates a common acoustic space that aural communications can share.

The concept of Scribblephone becomes even more exciting when a shared computer is added. The computer can aid and abet the interaction between people, or it can be used in person-to-computer communication. Both prospects are exciting, but more is known about the latter case.

Since the ultimate bind in any really large communication system that involves storage is the finite size of that storage medium, the limited bandwidth requirement of the Scribblephone type of terminal makes it very practical. Recent broadbank transmission developments completely ignore the storage size and cost constraint. This constraint must be recognized if inexpensive personal services providing individual interaction between people and their automata are to be realized. Storage costs must be kept as low as possible if we wish to make such services effective in addressing the wealth creating potential of ordinary citizens. This point is basic and crucial. Material for use with intelligent graphic terminals like Scribblephone will always occupy much less storage space than television type material.

The digitization of the common telephone network means that in time, facilities will exist that permit the widespread and massive use of such communication devices. The important thing is that this new world can be entered gently, without prohibitive expenditures on communications facilities before the first installation can occur. For once, the universe, usually perverse, is unfolding in a reasonable fashion.

Either of these particular technological developments, by itself, is of little significance when assessed by the technique described above. It is only when combined, and together combined with the further notions of widely available computing power and storage, that an exciting potential is apparent. Even then, the manner in which this is done, the way it is coupled into the society, is critical.

Community Retrieval Television

"Speech 73", a most exciting conference, was held in the very large auditorium at Seneca College in Toronto. During the speeches, the excitement of the audience was electric. As a test of the impact of the "vibrations" from the other members of the audience, I stepped out of the hall and listened to the proceedings over the very adequate sound system that was distributing the talks throughout the building. The change in impact was phenomenal; the speech sounded like any other prosaic presentation. I re-entered the auditorium, and the excitement was there again! A mere glance about the hall confirmed that the speaker was saying important things. Out in the corridor, the mechanical loudspeaker ground on and on to a totally disinterested environment.

Jane Jacobs, in *The Death and Life of Great American Cities,* identifies the common sidewalk as being essential to urban life. She devotes the first ninety pages to establishing the importance of sidewalks. Safe participation in an action arena where the level of involvement is largely under the participant's control seems to be the underlying characteristic of her "sidewalk". She is a lucid writer, and makes a very strong case for the kinds of interaction that a sidewalk encourages.

The growing popularity and the rapidly escalating budgets associated with sports spectaculars that are viewed over closed circuit television in arenas or other large auditoriums suggests that the same program delivered right into the home might be less dynamic and appealing. Perhaps part of the utility of attending such an event may stem from being with kindred souls; from knowing, feeling and sharing their enthusiasm. A smaller scale example can be found in the annual Grey Cup parties held in peoples' homes, where friends gather to celebrate the final culmination of the football season in a communal way.

Now, what do all these things have in common? A concern for the shared feelings within large but loosely defined groups of people. The electronic media developed to date tend to keep us all in isolation, or at best in two-by-two dyads. To some degree, our television might be thought of as a sort of sidewalk, in that it gives us a kind of window on the world. However, there is absolutely no manner in which one can vary the degree of his participation, nor is there any way one can sense his neighbours' concerns.

The television-based services that are discussed today as being the "Systems of Tomorrow" do not make the prospects any brighter. The common variants of Pay TV deliver content to the individual users in isolation, each user being carefully protected from benefiting from the choice another viewer may have made. In these formats, the entire system revenue must be derived from the individual charges associated with users' requests for specific material.

These systems sustain no essential feeling of community. They neither encourage nor invite additional levels of commitment. They have as much social excitement as the hose leading from a gasoline pump; they are just a delivery system.

Some time ago, the structure for a television distribution system was described in the Business Planning Group of Bell Canada that had a different twist to the way the business software was assembled, a twist that inadvertently gave the system some very desirable social characteristics. When the idea was first put forth, it was viewed as a cheap means of introducing demand television services, where the customer could get what he wanted, on his demand. It was only after analyzing the proposal with the communications innovation assessment technique that the significance of this particular proposal began to emerge. In describing the concept, we will follow its chronological development. However, recognize that, as you read, you will be asked to absorb ideas that took about a year or more to be accepted by even the concept champions. In short, this system is a sleeper; and like Vodka, hits you only after you may have prematurely dismissed it as insignificant!

Private Delivery Demand Systems need additional equipment over and beyond a conventional CATV system, to constrain the customer's normally free-roving television receiver to the particular material he ordered. The cost of this additional equipment is a further burden on an already dicey proposition. So, the proposal was to merely delete the privacy equipment, and try to live with the result.

The business software that was developed to accompany this stripped down demand system involved a monthly fee that gave the viewer access to all the delivery channels. One channel was devoted to the display of a schedule of what was happening and was about to happen on the remaining channels. This channel can be used for the "development of a market" for particular content. Supposing "Shallow Nostril" costs $350 per performance; through a form of public auction, such an amount could be cajoled out of the audience. Various schemes based on this theme could be used to permit the showing of very expensive, general interest material, while yet not denying the opportunity for the showing of low cost material of special interest to particular small audiences.

When a viewer wishes to make a specific fetch, chosen from the catalogue of possibilities, he telephones in his request, and it is scheduled at the next appropriate time. If the system should be lightly loaded, then his request would be shown immediately, for everyone to see. Otherwise, a suitable time would be negotiated. This new selection would be added to the list of performances displayed on the schedule channel.

A fetch charge is to be made for each request. Here is where the first significant advantage of leaving off the privacy equipment appears: the charge for that specific fetch need not be nearly so high as in the private delivery system. A portion of the monthly subscription fee from all users goes to defray the cost of this, and every, fetch.

The charge per fetch is a function of the subsidy that can be derived from the subscription fees. With a large number of subscribers, and a small number of channels, the bulk of the income for the service is generated by the subscription fees, and not by the fetch charges. The significance of this point is driven home by a study done by Walter S. Baer of S.R.I., wherein he noted that the library content costs alone make demand retrieval TV systems virtually impossible. He did not know about this simple variant.

The stripped down TV demand delivery system breaks one of the greatest dilemmas in the demand business. Everyone wants access to everything, but doesn't want to pay very much for it. People won't pay enough to attract content of any significance. That being the case, the library quality falls, and so the incentive to use the library also falls. Quality attracts usage, and usage attracts quality. There must be continual pump priming to keep this going. That's what the subscription fee is all about.

There is another subtlety in this stripped down demand system. This second benefit relates to the loading on the system's channels. Clearly, the system operator would like to run with all channels loaded, and maybe even a little overloaded, giving a delay of up to an hour or so for a fetch. Simple fetch pricing strategies tend to keep the channels just loaded.

The argument for this statement runs as follows: light system loading is obvious to the user who glances at the schedule channel, or flips through the spectrum of channels. He can easily see that material can be ordered for immediate delivery. On the other hand, when the system is fully loaded, a request must be scheduled. As the loading increases, there is less likelihood that the subscriber can achieve a satisfactory match with the system's timetable. So here we have a situation where the probability of additional immediate load being presented to the system falls sharply as the system becomes fully loaded. This produces a strong tendency toward having the system optimally loaded at all times. Additional discriminatory pressures can be built into the pricing policy to further enhance this characteristic, or to develop any other patterning that might be desired. Since each fetch is, in effect, a bargaining situation, prices for a fetch could go up and down like elevators without detracting from the overall revenue.

When this system was modeled on the laboratory computer, we discovered that as few as four hundred users could be enough to make it viable. However, if the creators of the library's content were looking to this medium for their sole support, then more than half a million subscribers, to systems of this type, would be needed. At this level and beyond, a significant business can be supported in the area of making specific content for these stripped down demand systems. Until this level is reached, content would be rented, bought, or accepted on consignment from television and motion picture sources or other information suppliers, so that the content costs would be differential rather than total.

As time went on, more and more good things began to emerge. The notion of varying levels of participation that is essential to Jane Jacobs' sidewalk was recognized. Since it costs a couple of dollars to make a fetch, one might try watching for a while, looking at what one's neighbours have requested. Of course, there is no way to find out who ordered what; one only knows that someone in his community ordered what he is seeing. He knows that the selection was probably made by someone just like himself. Now his courage builds. He reaches for the library listing, and contemplates a higher level of participation. Whether or not he makes a fetch is up to him. He can dicker with the librarian. If he wants it cheap, he can order it for 6 a.m. next Tuesday. His level of participation is set by his own decisions.

By watching this "electronic sidewalk", a viewer can get a flavour of his community, for all the material being shown has been selected by his fellow citizens. The content is totally the result of the choice of those viewing it — real community television!

A viewer can order for reshowing an interesting program that he tuned in on by chance, because the ordering information is still showing on the schedule channel. If he is really excited, he can order a scheduled showing, and suggest to his friends that they watch, in case they may be similarly moved. This is consensus building, and it is positive consensus, not that negative "Don't do this . . . Don't do that . . ." kind that permeates our present mass media.

Just as material from a video recorder or a film projector can be shown on this system, so sequences generated by computer can be shown. It is a very simple task to accommodate content that is generated, edited, and stored in a computer, for this can be played out through a conversion unit to generate the television signal required for distribution. A five minute summary of the latest stockmarket news, complete with charts and graphs, is an example of the content that might be presented in this fashion. Clearly, the computer file can be updated and edited very easily, making this a kind of program material that is always changing.

Instantaneous electronic television viewer polling can develop a high level of viewer involvement if the program content has been specially designed, and contains branches that are chosen as a result of the data collected by the polling system. This is particularly easy to automate where the content material is computer based. The program sequence, once initiated, can run automatically, with polls called for by the controlling computer. Program branching decisions would be based on the compilations of viewer responses performed by the polling computer. The program content for such productions could range from simple alpha-numeric material through to animated cartoons with accompanying sound, all computer generated and controlled. As part of the conventional practice for material of this sort, the results of the poll could be shown in detail, giving the viewer a sense of the magnitude of the response, as well as its direction. In this way, the viewer can be aware of the magnitude of the viewing audience together with its opinions and feelings.

The combination of Community Retrieval Television and electronic polling begins to approach some of the scenarios depicted at the beginning of this chapter. The viewer can participate in the generation of shared feelings in a large but loosely defined group. Here, he can sense the pulse of the group's feelings. This combination of services is the most significant new positive consensus generating communications innovation now known. The social and economic importance of this combination is very difficult to estimate in any "hard" fashion, for innovations of this type directly address the fundamental wealth creating processes of the society. The theoretical work we have done suggests that this kind of service is vitally important.

Whether the viewer chooses an intense level of

participation as exemplified by the computer-polling kind of material, or elects to share the more conventional selections of his neighbours, the effect is the same. As he roams through the channels, he can feel the presence of his fellow citizens. There is a feeling of community, for he feels the effects of his neighbours.

It is a simple step to introduce an input facility to allow the users of the system to create their own library content contributions. Since this material would be available on request, it wouldn't be necessary to put one's all into a single, ephemeral appearance. Better content should evolve from such an approach to developing community inputs to television. Montreal's Videographe is living proof of the viability of meaningful public participation in content generation.

Since the material, once ordered, is probably viewed by more than just the person ordering the showing, there is a chance that content deserving a wider acclaim will develop that acclaim, while the poor stuff will just move back further into colder and colder storage areas until it is finally returned to the author as having no further use. Continued occupancy of storage space should require that the author pay for that space; the clunkers will get weeded out, or generate revenue.

Eventually, the library that serves a particular community will become some kind of intellectual map of that community. When a stranger moves into the community, he can consult the library content popularity data to get a particular insight into his new community.

Community Retrieval Television — it is a stripped down, demand, retrieval system for television material that began life with an apology, but now looks happier and healthier than its parents.

Conclusion

In either of these systems, the solution to Bar-Hillel's conundrum is by way of increasing the pluralisms by opening the game as wide as possible, and giving prizes to the successful contenders. It is reminiscent of how the British solved the longitude problem by offering a twenty thousand pound prize which evoked a solution from a humble carpenter's son. Bar-Hillel's conundrum may be a similar problem, and may also need a carpenter's son for solution.

In both these systems, computers can play a part in creating, from stored algorithms, material for use on the systems. The automatic creation of information by computers, tailored to suit each individual user, has been identified as a wealth generator of significance approaching the industrial revolution. In Japan, Yoneji Masuda is attempting to develop a new economic theory to demonstrate, explain, and substantiate this concept.

Survival of our society may depend on shifting our economy from a largely consumption driven one toward a communications driven one. The sublimation of consumption into communications may become a necessity. This can occur only if we produce several new and exciting communications media that really address the basic wealth creating processes of such a society. This communications innovation assessment technique is a beginning. The two systems described above are possibilities that will need some considerable research before we can be sure they will produce the effects we seek. They have been shaped by interacting with that assessment technique. It is naive to think these either are fully thought out, or are the only configurations that will work. We need a lot more work in this important area of designing communications media that are really revolutionary in a basic social and economic sense. However, one thing seems clear: these new systems will have to be such that ordinary people will want to, and can, create material that is saleable to other people.

Authorship, in such an environment, represents the creation of a block of capital, for the royalties received by an author, for the use of his material, look like interest payments. This represents a radical economic break-through, for it enables the direct conversion of labour into capital. Since ordinary people without wealthy connections or institutional subservience could avail themselves of this process, it would greatly increase the opportunity for everyone to become a practising capitalist — "convivial capitalism" in action!

Investment in telecommunications tools that are available for public use is fundamentally different from investment in either primary or secondary industry. Communications tools are a public good, whereas the investment in tools devoted to the consumption ethic by their very nature are constrained to be private goods. The conviviality of this potential communications revolution stems from this "public good" aspect of proper investments in communica-tions technology. Much research may be needed to really understand the processes involved, so that we can move toward the goals of "convivial capitalism" and the sublimation of consumption into communications.

Surely such goals are worth some considerable research. The hardware exists, we know what the elements are, but we do not know how to pattern them to really improve our prospects of dealing with our problem / opportunity. Good research clearly is needed in this area.

Man and Media

H. MARSHALL McLUHAN

Man and Media

H. MARSHALL McLUHAN

When I was in Barcelona a few weeks ago, I had a translator who was very good, and listening to him I noticed something that might be of some relevance. You cannot translate jokes into another language. Now the reason is that a joke requires a hidden ground of grievances, for which the joke is only a figure sitting in front. You remember the Streakers? They had a kind of grievance and it's now called "just a passing fanny". But the grievance behind the Streakers' performance cannot be translated. You cannot verbalize the kinds of grievances that prompted the Streakers to go into action. Even the simplest jokes cannot be provided with a ground that makes them plausible.

So I had in mind to tell my Spanish audience a few of our Newfie stories by way of introducing them to Canada. I thought of stories like the one about the Newfie who went into the bank to cash a cheque. When asked to identify himself, he produced a pocket mirror, looked in it, and said, "That's me, all right."

And there is the one about the Newfie who was asked by a sociologist inquiring at the door, "Do you have any other brothers and sisters?" He said, "Yes, I have a brother at Harvard." "Oh, what's he studying at Harvard?" "He's not studying at Harvard. They're studying him."

Or these:

On top of a Newfie ladder there is written on the rung, "Stop here."

On the bottom of every Newfie beer bottle there is the instruction, "Open other end."

How would a Newfie have handled Watergate? The same way.

And so on. Now, why are these Newfie jokes? What is this grievance we have against Newfies? If we didn't have a grievance, there would not be any stories.

The Newfie stories happen to be our kind of bundle at the moment, but the same is true in any other language. These jokes do, or try to, cross borders and move from one area to another. Jokes are themselves a very important form of communication and they reflect certain grievances and irritations which everybody feels. And yet, very little notice is given to them.

In Paris a few months ago, I was told the joke about the man who felt that he was alienated and alone in the world. He went to the roof of his high-rise building and jumped off. As he was passing the floor of his apartment, he heard the telephone ringing. The telephone reminded him there was still somebody in the world besides himself.

Now that is a sick joke. Sick jokes are a new form of grievance and just why they should have their vogue is worth looking into.

In Moscow they tell the story about the attempt to set up an American-style nightclub. This nightclub flopped, and a committee was formed to examine the situation. Questions were asked. How about the food? And the managers explained, "We had French chefs and cuisine and the best wine and good prices, very reasonable prices." How about the decor, the layout? The managers replied, "Well, we had Italian designers with Hollywood consultants." And how about the girls? "They were absolutely tops, every one of them Party members since 1917." So you can see where the grievance is in Russia.

You cannot have a joke without a grievance. The fast pace in our world has led to the development of the "one-liner", the abbreviated joke. The one-liner is for people of very short attention span, who won't stay around long enough for you to tell them a story. You have to work fast. You flip in with a single gag — in one ear and out the other. There is the one-liner about Zeus, who says to his fellow god, Narcissus, "Watch yourself." Another one — "You cannot see the writing on the wall until your back is up against it." Or — "Politics is shooting from the lip." The list is simply endless.

These responses to grievance situations lead to much stronger reactions or statements, such as horror movies, vampire movies, and our general cult of horror. This is a response to situations of the media which people feel are involving them, imbedding them. *The Exorcist* is an account of how it feels to live in the electric age — how it feels to be completely taken over by alien forces and hidden powers. The viewer feels he has been obsessed or possessed.

And, of course, there is the one-liner, "If you do not pay your exorcist, you will be repossessed."

However, the drop-out is the figure of our time. He is the person who is trying to get in touch. When you get uptight, you have to let go in order to get back in touch. "To get in touch" is a strange phrase. When a wheel and an axle are playing along together, as long as there is a nice interval between the wheel and the axle, they are "in touch". When the interval gets too small or too big, they lose touch, the wheel is either "on the hot box", "uptight", or "seized up", or else "falls apart".

Keeping in touch requires this interplay, this interface, which is a kind of interval of response. Touch is actually not connection but interval. When you touch an object there is a little space between yourself and the object, a space which resonates. That is play — and without play, there cannot be any creative activity in any field at all.

This leads to the theme of violence as a response to situations in which you feel you have lost identity; situations in which you feel you have been ripped off by too rapid changes — where you have suddenly been flipped from one situation to another without warning and you are suddenly minus your identity. You don't know who you are. You don't know where you are. This leads to a response of violence.

Incidentally, in a public situation such as an ordinary football game, all persons present are nobodies. Even if you were sitting there with Charlie Chaplin, or the Duke of Edinburgh, they would be nobodies and you would be a nobody. Anybody at a ballgame is a nobody. Now what is the compensation that people expect for becoming nobodies? They expect violence. And so sport provides an organized, systematized form of violence which compensates the participants and the audience for being nobodies.

The nobody in real life is a person who becomes quite intractable, quite violent, as a way of rediscovering "Who am I?" and "How do I re-establish my image, myself, in this world?" Our popular forms of entertainment tend toward that direction. Whether it's westerns or whodunits or horror movies or just about any other kind of movie, these are movies in which people are questing for their identity. You may remember an episode in the novel *Passage to India* by E.M. Forster, in which Adela Quested encounters a strange figure in the Marabar caves. It is a moment for her of absolute horror. This encounter of a highly civilized person with an unknown force is a kind of interplay between the merely visual and the merely familiar and the hidden, echoing, resonating ghost-like world.

In our time, one of the strange things that is happening is not unrelated to that. Having come out of a very visual age with organized points of view, positions, jobs, attitudes, we are suddenly confronted with an instantaneous-simultaneous world in which there are no familiar boundaries. Moving from the old hardware world of the nineteenth century and industrial or first-world technology — the first-world technology of the familiar productive and industrial type — into a world of instant information and design and pattern is a flip from a visual world to an acoustic world. The main aspect of our simultaneous-instantaneous time is essentially acoustic, not visual, since no point-of-view is possible to the ear.

To the world of the simultaneous and the instantaneous there is no sequence. There is no logic. There is only the simultaneous-instantaneous burst breakthrough. I was once in a plane when it was struck by lightning. There was suddenly a bang and a flash and the stewardess casually said, "We have just been hit by lightning." This never had happened before to me, but apparently was a common occurrence to her. To a person who had not a clue as to what had happened it would be rather startling. But this very world of the instantaneous, the simultaneous, is the world in which we live.

What is called the "generation gap" represents a division between people who grew up in the visual era of the first world with its industrial complex — a world of jobs, of points-of-view, of policies and attitudes — and the children of those people, children who were raised in the acoustic simultaneous-instantaneous world of television. This had happened to a smaller degree in the 1920s with radio. The radio generation was somewhat alienated, dislocated; it was called the "lost generation" by Gertrude Stein. However, the radio generation remained relatively intact compared to the TV generation. Perhaps we should look further into that — the generation gap between parents who grew up in the old first world and their children who grew up in the fourth

world. The fourth world is the electric world that goes
around the first, second, and third worlds. The first world is
the industrial world of the nineteenth century. The second
world is Russian socialism. The third world is the rest of the
world where industrial institutions have yet to establish
themselves, and the fourth world is a world that goes around
all of them.

The fourth world is ours. It is the electric world, the
computer world, the instantaneous communication world.
The fourth world can come to Africa before the second or
first world. Radio came to Africa and began to penetrate
African institutions and psyches a long time ago. Radio
went to China and India long before anything else from the
West. The coming of the fourth world, the electric-instant-
aneous world, has been completely ignored by the
journalists and by the Marxists. Marx was a nineteenth-
century man, a hardware man of the first world only, who
knew nothing about electricity, nothing about the
instantaneous. He could not possibly know what might
happen in a fourth world, an instantaneous world of electric
information. His entire thought was based upon production
and distribution of product. His conviction was that if
everybody could have enough of everything, problems
would disappear. It never occurred to him that perhaps the
most important commodity in the twentieth century would
be information and not hardware products. Information is
not only our biggest business, but has become education
itself.

But I have digressed slightly. My main topic is "Man and
Media", a topic which relates to an aspect of media on
which I have been working a great deal lately. The preface
to a new book of mine begins, "All of man's artifacts, of
language, of laws, of ideas, hypotheses, tools, clothing,
computers — all of these are extensions of our physical
bodies." This power to extend ourselves was used as a theme

by Hans Haas in his book *The Human Animal*. In it he considers this human ability to create additional organs as an enormity from the evolution standpoint — an advance laden with unfathomable consequences. My own "Laws of the Media" are observations on the operation and effects of human artifacts on man and society, or, as Hans Haas notes, "a human artifact is not merely an implement for working upon something but an extension of our body effected by artificial additional organs to which, to a greater or lesser degree, we owe our civilization." Haas considers our bodily extensions as having these advantages: (a) they have no need of constant nourishment, thus they save energy; (b) they can be discarded or stored rather than carried around, a further saving of energy; (c) they are exchangeable, enabling man to specialize, to play many roles, so that when carrying a spear he can be hunter or when using a paddle he can move across the sea. All of these instruments can be shared communally. They can be made in any community by specialists, thus giving rise to handcraft skills.

Something overlooked by Hans Haas was the absence of biological or psychological means of coping with the effects of our own technological ingenuity in creating new organs. The problem is clearly indicated in Albert Simeons' *Man's Presumptuous Brain,* in which he says that, about half a million years ago, when man began slowly to embark upon the road to cultural advance, an entirely new condition developed. The use of implements and the control of fire introduced technologies which the cortex was able to use for purposes of living. However, these new situations or artifacts had no relationship whatever to the organization of the body and could therefore not be integrated into the functioning of the brainstem. The brainstem, or diencephalon, man's great regulating sentry or centre, continued to function just as if the artifacts were non-existent. But as the diencephalon is also the organ from which the instincts are generated, the earliest humans found themselves faced with a very old problem in a new garb. Their instinctive behaviour ceased to be appropriate in the new situations which the cortex created by using artifacts.

The new artificial environment that man began to build for himself at the dawn of culture made many of his animal reflexes useless. Simeons is saying that our natural responses to media and technology are irrelevant, that we cannot trust our instincts or our natural physical responses to new things. They will destroy us. How are we to bypass or offset the merely physical response to new technology and new environments created by new technology?

This problem has not been raised by anybody even though we have to live with it every day. Edgar Allan Poe's story "The Descent into the Maelstrom" had tremendous influence on the nineteenth century poets and symbolists like Baudelaire, Flaubert, and others. In this story, Poe imagines the situation in which a sailor, who has gone out on a fishing expedition, finds himself caught in a huge maelstrom or whirlpool. He sees that his boat will be sucked down into this thing. He begins to study the action of the storm, and observes that some things disappear and some things reappear. By studying those that reappear and attaching himself to one of them, he saves himself. Pattern recognition in the midst of a huge, overwhelming, destructive force is the way out of the maelstrom. The huge vortices of energy created by our media present us with similar possibilities of evasion of consequences, of destruction. By studying the patterns of the effects of this huge vortex of energy in which we are involved, it may be possible to program a strategy of evasion and survival.

Survival cannot be trusted to natural response or natural instinct since the brainstem is not provided with any means of responding to man-made environments. Our diencephalon, our huge evolutionary structure of nerves and brainstem, evolved over long periods of time and had ended its development long before the first technology. Long before fire or clothing, this brainstem had completed its programming. And so with the coming of fire and clothing and weapons, the brainstem was unable to respond relevantly to any of these artifacts. The artist's insights or perceptions seem to have been given to mankind as a providential means of bridging the gap between evolution and technology. The artist is able to program, or re-program, the sensory life in a manner which gives us a navigational chart to get out of the maelstrom created by our own ingenuity. The role of the artist in regard to man and the media is simply survival.

There is a passage in Anthony Storr's *The Human Aggression* in which he observes that it is obviously true that most bomber pilots are, morally, no better or worse than other men. The majority, given a can of petrol and told to pour it over a child of three and ignite it, would probably disobey the order. Yet, put that same decent man in an airplane a few hundred feet above a village, and he will kill without compunction. He will drop high explosives and napalm, inflicting appalling pain and injury on men, women, and children. The distance between him and the people he is bombing makes them into an impersonal target — no longer human beings like himself, with whom he can identify.

This is a characteristic situation. That bomber pilot is really very much like the person introducing new technology using ordinary human business resources and an existing institutional means. No one ever considers what will be the impact or the effect of what he does when he pulls that trigger. Quite apart from the use of weaponry at a distance, there are the effects of changes in man himself which result from using his own devices to create environments of service.

Any new service environment such as that created by railways or motorcars, or telegraph or radio, deeply modify the very nature and image of the people who use them. Radical changes of identity happening in very sudden, brief intervals of time have proved more deadly and destructive to human values than were wars fought with hardware weapons. In the electric age the alteration of human identity by new service environments of information have left whole populations without personal or community values to a degree that far exceeds the effects of food and fuel and energy shortages. I am suggesting that the Club of Rome is really talking to the old nineteenth century situation of quantity and hardware and ignoring completely the effect of software information on the human psyche. The rip-off of human psychic resources by new media may far exceed the dangers involved in energy shortages from hardware.

I am going to introduce a new survival approach in my forthcoming book on laws of the media and I hope that readers will offer many improvements to this method. In the meantime, I suggest that it is possible to notice, to understand, the effects of any technology, whether new or old, by applying these four questions to the situation:

1. What does the technology amplify, enhance, or enlarge?
2. What does it obsolesce?
3. What does it retrieve or bring back from a distant past? (Probably something that was scrapped earlier.)
4. What does it flip or suddenly reverse into when pushed to its limits?

I will give you a few examples of this pattern — these four phases or stages in the development of any artifact whatever.

I have in front of me in isolation from other things a *camera*. By its snapshotting quality it enhances aggression

and private power over people. It obsolesces privacy. It
retrieves the past as present; it brings back the big game
hunter. Bringing him home alive means bringing people
home alive; photographic journalism is very big game
hunting. It flips into the public domain.

The *zipper* — the homely zipper. It amplifies a grip, the
clasp. It obsolesces the button, the snap. It retrieves
long-flowing robes, easy to manage. It reverses into velcro
drape, no clasps, no buttons, no zipper, no closure at all.

The *clock* amplifies work — until the clock was invented,
what we call work was almost impossible to organize. It
obsolesces leisure. It retrieves history as art form by fixed
chronology — immeasurable, sequential chronology capable of visual time as measured by the clock. It reverses
when pushed all the way into the eternal present, a nowness.

Electric media in general amplify information, range,
and scope, pushing information into a service environment
by simultaneity. Electric media obsolesce the visual, the
connected, the logical, the rational. They retrieve the
subliminal, audile, tactile dialogue, involvement. They
bring back, rather reverse, finally, all hardware into
software. The motorcar is worth only a few bucks in
hardware terms; it is worth many millions in software terms
of design. And consider electric speeds. The sender is sent.
The sender goes on the air and is instantaneously
everywhere without a body. Electricity creates the angelic or
discarnate being of electronic man who has no body. When
you are on the telephone, you are in New York, or here,
simultaneously, and so is the person you are speaking to,
minus the body. The implication of discarnate, disembo-
died existence in an information world is one for which our
educational system has not quite prepared us.

The familiar *elevator,* originally designed to take people
down into the depths of the earth, enhances speed of access
and distance of depth, creating undergound cities. Its

original use was in mining; the first underground cities were mines. It obsolesces staircases and ladders. It retrieves hidden treasure, minerals, and secrets. It flips into high-rise, skyscraper, and new fractions and egalitarianism of the elevator.

Money simply speeds up transactions. It is a technology for homogenizing the information situation among participants. Therefore, it speeds up transactions; you can move goods at very high speeds with money. It obsolesces barter. It retrieves potlatch or the conspicuous expenditure and flips into credit, which is not money.

Instant replay enhances awareness of the cognitive process. It obsolesces the representational, the chronological, in that it doesn't matter in what sequence the events occurred. It retrieves meaning. You can have the meaning in instant replay without the experience. This is a rather startling aspect of the instant replay: you can have the meaning, the structure, minus the experience of the event. And it flips into corporate pattern recognition, which is easily associated with tradition. The instant replay is, perhaps, the most remarkable development of our time, and one of the most profound and metaphysical.

This pattern of four aspects of change — enhancing, obsolescing, retrieving, and flipping — happens to be the pattern of metaphor. All metaphors have these four aspects. All metaphors are figure / ground in ratio to figure/ground. There are four parts: a figure in the ground and a figure in the ground. They are not connected. They are in ratio.

Metaphors are in. All technologies have these four aspects. I was gradually forced to conclude that all human extensions are uttering or outerings of our own beings and are literally linguistic in character. Whether it is your shoes or a walking stick, a zipper or a bulldozer, all of these forms are linguistic in structure and are outerings or utterings of man's own being. They have their own syntax and grammar as much as any verbal form. This was an unexpected result of looking at these innovations structurally, not with an intent to discover anything except individual structures. Eventually I realized that these structures are literally linguistic; there is no difference between hardware and software, between verbal and non-verbal technology in terms of this linguistic character or sharing.

This suggests, therefore, that man's technology is the most human thing about him. Our hardware — mechanisms of all types: spectacles, microphones, paper, shoes — all of these forms are utterly verbal and linguistic in character and are utterly human. The word "utter" is from "outer" and "outering" is the nature of technology. Extension of bodily organs into the environment is a form of utterance or expression.

There is, therefore, a completely intelligible character and pattern in these outerings or utterings. In a book by Martin Heidegger titled *The Origin of the Work of Art,* there is a wonderful passage in which he is talking about a pair of peasant shoes painted by Van Gogh.

> We shall choose a well-known painting by Van Gogh, who painted such shoes several times. But what is there to see here? Everyone knows what shoes consist of if they are not wooden or bast shoes. There will be leather soles and uppers joined together by thread and nails. Such gear serves to clothe the feet depending on the use to which the shoes are put; whether for work or in the field or for dancing, matter and form will differ.

Now, such statements, no doubt, only explicate what we already know. The equipmental quality of equipment consists in its usefulness. But what about this usefulness itself? In conceiving it do we not already conceive along with it the equipmental character of equipment? In order to succeed in doing this, must we not look out for useful equipment at its best?

The peasant woman wears her shoes in the field — only here are they what they are — and they are all the more genuinely so the less the peasant woman thinks about the shoes while she is at work or looks at them at all or is even aware of them. She stands and walks in them. That is how shoes actually serve. It is in this process of the use of equipment that we must actually encounter the character of equipment.

As long as we only imagine a pair of shoes in general, or look at the empty unused shoes as they merely stand there in the picture, we shall never discover what the equipmental being of equipment really is. From Van Gogh's painting, we cannot even tell where these stand. There is nothing surrounding this pair of shoes, no ground in which they might belong, only an undefined space. I would call that space an acoustic, resonating space. There are not even clods of soil from the field sticking to them — they are a pair of peasant shoes and nothing more.

And yet, from the dark opening of worn insides of the shoes, the toilsome tread of the worker stands forth. In the stiffly rugged heaviness of the shoes, there is the accumulated tenacity of the slow trudge through the far-spreading and ever-uniform fields swept by raw wind. On the leather lie the dampness and richness of the soil. Under the soles slides the loneliness of the fieldpath as evening falls. In these shoes vibrates the silent call of the earth; its quiet gift of ripening grain; its unexplained self-refusal in the fallow desolation in the wintery field. This equipment is pervaded by uncomplaining anxiety as to the certainty of bread, the wordless joy of having once more withstood want, the trembling before the impending childbed and shivering at the surrounding menace of death. This equipment belongs to the earth and it is protected in the world of the peasant woman. From out of this protected belonging, the equipment rises to its resting within itself.

But perhaps it is only in the picture that we notice all these things about the shoes. The peasant woman, on the other hand, simply wears them. If only this simple wearing were so simple. When she takes off her shoes, late in the evening, in deep but healthy fatigue, and reaches out for them again in the still dim dawn, or passes by them on the day of rest, she knows all this without noticing or reflecting. The equipmental quality of the equipment consists indeed in its usefulness. But this usefulness rests in the abundance of an essential being of the equipment we call reliability.

By virtue of this reliability the peasant woman is made privy to the silent fall of the earth. By virtue of the reliability of the equipment she is sure of her world. Now the artist translates the hardware or equipment into another mode for contemplation. Equipment is here, and reliability.

Another idea that I would like to develop here is that of organized ignorance as an untouched resource. We are always trying to translate ignorance into knowledge and flip it on its back, as it were. But perhaps there is a way to organize human ignorance as a positive resource, in this day of the mass audience created by electric media. The word "mass" simply means simultaneous. Mass-man is man existing simultaneously in the same world. It is a matter of speed, not of numbers. It doesn't matter if it's six, or six million. If it is simultaneous, it is mass. This is part of Einstein's theories.

Now, suppose that we put questions to that mass, through electronic media, concerning the problems of our time; suppose that top researchers in various fields, in biology and chemistry and physics and town-planning and so on, ask these questions; suppose they were to go to the broadcasting studios and present, not their knowledge, but their hang-ups. Suppose they were to tell the mass, in the most succinct, atavistic, and structured form, where the difficulties are. Robert Oppenheimer used to say, "There are kids playing here on the street who could solve some of my toughest problems in physics because they have modes of perception that I lost long ago."

Out in the mass audience, every single possible mode of perception exists unawares. But how do we tap that resource? I suggest that one possibility would be to take these highly specialist problems to this mass of untutored, non-specialist people. There is always one man in a million for whom any problem is not a problem at all. For a long time mathematicians used to pose as unanswerable the problem, "How far can you go into a forest?" One day some infant simply said, "Halfway." And that is the answer; after that, you are coming out.

And it was an eight-year-old child who invented the cybernetic mechanism, called the governor, on a steam engine. It happened this way. He worked on a steamboat, and it was his job to pull the steamcock with a string. As the wheel went around, so the big piston went around. But he wanted to play marbles, so he tied the string to the flywheel and invented the first automatic governing mechanism in the world.

I suggest you will find historically that the greatest inventions were made anonymously by nobodies for whom there was no problem; they simply used common sense. All problems, when solved, in retrospect seem to have been easy. Why are they so hard when we are looking ahead at them? I suggest that to the untutored mass out there, all of the existing problems of the specialist are not problems at all. That is to say, what constitutes opacity when looking ahead is the misdirected knowledge of the specialist which shines in the face of the questor or pursuer. When a flashlight shines in your face you cannot see a thing. Now the specialist does that all the time; the flashlight of his specialty shines in his face, obscuring the answer to his problem. But there is always one man in a million for whom there is no problem. This feature of organized ignorance is a typical flip of the situation in which we live and I am going to note a few other situations which are similar.

At jet speed there is no rearview mirror. What does one see in the rearview mirror at motor car speed? In the jet plane at jet speed, there is no rearview mirror and nothing can be seen. What do you see in the rearview mirror of a motor car? The foreseeable future: you don't see what went past, you see what is coming! It is obvious, isn't it? The phrase "rearview mirror" tells you that you are looking at something that went past, but in fact, you never do; all you can look at in the rearview mirror is, literally, the foreseeable future.

Now, at the speed of light, there is no foreseeable future. You are there — literally. It does not matter what situation you choose to consider. There is literally no possible future. You are already there the moment you name the situation. That is why in our age there are no goals. That is the reason for the Streakers' antics: they are protesting the disappearance of goals. Where are we going? We are all dressed up with no place to go. We think we have taken all the right school courses, studied the right subjects, but now it all seems pointless. Where do we go from here?

Literally, there are no goals at the speed of light, but there are roles. At the speed of light, instead of having a job or an objective, you have to determine for yourself a totally new pattern, a new function in the world. And your new function is that of role-playing, which consists in taking on a whole variety of jobs at once. An ordinary mother in a big family has many jobs to perform. So does a farmer. We consider them to be role-players. A farmer doesn't have a job and a mother doesn't have a job. She has a role, a very involved, complicated one.

At the speed of light all of us will find ourselves involved more and more in role-playing. Ralph Nader at Convocation Hall recently made some very commonsense observations about this very matter. He pointed out that students in the university were in a very, very wonderful position to do research into all aspects of the existing environment, as they have immediate access to all the knowledge of that environment. What they do not have is guidance on how to get at that knowledge. He said students should be using their own courses and their own free time, remembering that they have much more free time now than they ever will have again as long as they live. This free time can be used for all sorts of hobbies and research into public administration and into every aspect of community service. He himself, of course, is a great example of just that. Amateur (meaning non-specialist) research into existing public services is a possible good use of free time of university students while they are still taking courses. There is not a university course that cannot be turned toward the investigation of existing public services. Once a student decides to investigate (and that is role-playing, by the way) using his courses at the university to do so, he becomes a role-player. He assumes, as Ralph Nader has assumed for himself, a role. He does not have a job but he does have a role.

Role-playing is the new electronic form of job-holding; it is replacing job-holding. It does require a kind of reallocation of energies. At the speed of light, all the old hardware pattern-recognition is useless. Without the awareness of the pattern, that is, if you do not know the new pattern in the instant replay, you will be unable to make any use of it — and so on.

Hieronymous Bosch has a series of paintings which are currently popular and are considered to be examples of psychological horror. Bosch simply took the images of the preceding time, the time just before his own, and pushed them physically or pictorially through the images of his own time. By taking these medieval icons and pushing them into the new pictorial space of the Renaissance, a point-of-view space, he created horror. We are now living in a world where all the old pictorial space and all the point-of-view space of visual man is being inundated by the icons and the corporate images of advertising and huge public services.

All these contemporary electric forms have many, many medieval characteristics. They are acoustic; they are not visual. As these acoustic forms go riding through the old visual forms of our establishment, we get a confrontation of horror. This world of interplay leads, I think, to the world of the vampire movies, to the world of horror films, and is a kind of catharsis for that discomfort created by the clash of worlds. The totally alien and incompatible character of the visual and the acoustic which Bosch in the fifteenth century presented as horror is presented in our time, too, as horror, but in the opposite way. The scenery is moving in, or is arranged, in the opposite pattern.

Joseph Conrad's world possesses this kind of image. In *Heart of Darkness,* Conrad faces a situation in Africa in which a group of Europeans are trying to exploit the ivory trade, and at the same time trying to civilize the natives. This is a peculiar interplay. Mark Slade has written about it in a recent essay in *Mosaic Magazine,* in which he says: "Man lives in the flicker, Man lives in the flicker." This comment was coined by Joseph Conrad in *Heart of Darkness.* He wrote the story about the same time moving pictures were first beamed out of a synthetic heart of darkness. These electrically controlled images gave man twenty-four flickers a second to live in; moving pictures flash by at twenty-four frames per second. It is in the flicker that man seizes a meaning for himself. But for Conrad's character, the flickers race out of control in a riot of sensory inputs. Moving images also offer a riot of flickers which tumble after one another. The effect in its most extreme form is something like being tickled to death.

Conrad confronts this inner-outer problem in this passage: "A common error is to regard the civilizing process and the humanizing process as synonymous." We have long supposed that civilization and humanizing are the same thing. Civilization is a product of literacy, and humanizing may or may not be. A correlation between the two is yet to be demonstrated.

Another passage from *Heart of Darkness* reads: "A first glance at the place was enough to let you see the flabby devil was running that show." To be forced to return to an examination of our own origins may not be such a bad thing. What can be claimed for literature and civilization is that they are euphemisms for hope. But hope for a better existence, for self-knowledge and understanding, could be realized, so it seemed to Western man, by severing his ties with the tangled undergrowth of myth and superstition. He erected a greasy pole, the alphabet, on which he hoped to shinny out of the swamps.

The civilized man imagines that he is going to help the native by stripping off the native's world of myth and legend, ritual, and superstition. The paradox is that in the electric age we ourselves are moving into, returning to, the acoustic world of simultaneous involvement and awareness, experiencing the surfacing of the subliminal life. When all things are simultaneous (that is, at the speed of light), the things that are ordinarily put aside into the subconscious simply come up into the conscious. This is the meaning of Freud's *Interpretation of Dreams*. The surfacing of man's subconscious came with the telegraph, the telephone, radio, and then TV and other electric media. It is impossible to sublimate or keep anything hidden at that speed. So we have to invent a new concept of civilization and humanizing in order to live at the speed of light. We had imagined that we could simply strip off the acoustic culture of these primitives, or these natives, in order to civilize them, but the same stripping off of our civilization is taking place at the same time, by means of our new electric technology. We are losing our civilization even faster than we stripped off the institutions of the Indians and the Africans.

Commonly known, too, is the fact that many societies recoil from the very idea of being wrenched from their primitive reality. This is one of the big protests coming out of Africa right now. Africans do not want to be civilized. They do not want to become private people. They want to retain their corporate social institutions. Usually they have to be taken from them at the cost of massive slaughter. To force these people above their hereditary food supply standard, to tear away their mythic roots, to wipe out the only survival pattern they knew, constituted the worst conceivable betrayal of sacred trust. The sacrifice of human life was another.

Mark Slade is simply talking about this paradox that we experience in moving into the acoustic world or simultaneous electric world, in which the world of the alphabet and of one thing at a time is not easy to maintain. Civilized Western man developed because of an alphabet which gave him a non-acoustic grasp of his world. He translated the whole of Homer and the acoustic encyclopaedia into visual form and developed a whole new set of equipment of analysis and rational drive, goals, patterns. Euclid's theories were invented and new kinds of visual space discovered at the same time. This visual man with his rational aggressive drive for goals was invented by this visual alphabet.

This visual alphabet to which we all are still subjected, under the name of literacy, is totally incompatible with instantaneous-simultaneous images of electric time. That does not mean one is good and one is bad. It just means they have completely different characteristics, and the values that are secreted by or brought to us by either form are not necessarily compatible any more.

I am not offering any solutions. I think that once you know where the structure of the problem is, it may be possible to hit upon solutions. But it certainly is very difficult to find solutions without awareness of where the problem is. I previously mentioned the novel by Forster, in which confrontation between the highly visual westerner Adela Quested and her oriental guests or hosts takes place in the Marabar Caves. She almost loses her mind as her strong visual sensitivity or bias encounters the acoustic world of the ear and the corporate non-individual society of the East. This is the situation in which all of us in the fourth world are now engaged.

Mass Communication in Canadian Society

DAVIDSON DUNTON

Mass Communication in Canadian Society

DAVIDSON DUNTON

Just sixty years ago, the only means of mass communication in Canada was daily newspapers. Then came radio, followed in the last quarter century by a series of revolutions in communication at a speed the world has never known before. Among them has been television.

In September 1952 came that amazing day, the start of television. Television since has produced, as we predicted then, enormous changes in Canadian society. Later came the addition of UHF and colour, followed by the magna kind of developments possible from satellites and from smaller things like transistors, making much more intimate, easily transportable, smaller equipment available to do efficient work.

Recently has come the development, particularly important for Canada, of cable television. As recently as ten years ago the experts were laughing it off; they said nothing much would come of it. But a few pioneers, particularly in this country, the United States, and Britain, persisted; and we now have in Canada a new household delivery system of very great importance.

During these years of the development of visual communication, FM radio was also growing, slowly at first, then vigorously during the sixties. There has also been the continuing development of computers, not just as calculating machines, but as agents of communication. We are certainly in the midst of a communication revolution.

And let us not forget, in our attention to the broadcasting media, that there have been technical changes in the print media as well. The sixties saw the development of typesetting by tape and at a remote distance by wire. Now there are newspapers in this country that are produced without metallic type at all. They use type which is arranged by a computer, then photographed, and reproduced on the cylinders of an offset press. So there is developing, even in the print sector, a marriage between wires, electronic channels, and computers.

Notwithstanding predictions to the contrary, in my own view the print media still have a very good future. Although information in print can be understood only by translating the characters which spell out the words of a language, there is nevertheless a great deal of convenience to it. Suppose that, by some quirk of technology, computers and wire transmission had been invented before the book and the printing press. People would have begun storing and retrieving information from computers. They would then have got computer printouts. Next, they would have found it useful to staple the printouts together and fasten them into hard covers in order to preserve them — and the modern book would have been invented. Such books would have been considered a great technological development for storing information. In fact, we are now producing some books by just that kind of system.

Of all the developments that are now taking place and that may occur in the next quarter century, the most important thing is the multiplication of the number of channels of mass communication. There are many more means of getting messages to people's homes than there were even twenty-five years ago. The development of many more channels of communication, whatever their forms, has great significance for society, because this development results in increasing specialization in different media or sub-media.

For example, in areas where there are a number of television and radio channels, services that are not linked to major networks tend to appeal to selected audience segments within society. While a number of general interest magazines have failed in recent years in both the U.S. and Canada, at the same time a number of special interest magazines have developed to serve particular needs of specific audiences.

Another very interesting development is the growth of community newspapers under the coverage of large metropolitan dailies. People in communities within some of our great modern conurbations, while still looking at television and taking the big daily newspapers, also read local printed media. Presumably, these small papers tell them more about their particular, small community. This trend toward specialized functions of different media is a healthy one that is going to continue.

This trend to specialization does, however, pose some questions for the big media organizations. If there are an increasing number of vehicles serving specific interests very well, whether those other vehicles be electronic or print, daily newspapers and network television services will have to consider more and more carefully to what extent their services should be directed to the mass audience, and to what extent they too, perhaps in different segments of their paper or at different times of day, should very specifically serve particular interest groups. Of course, there have long been some trends in this direction, especially in network radio and television and in the special departments and sections of daily newspapers. It is inevitable, and probably to the benefit of the public, that there will be not only specialization of services but increasing division and departmentalization of function in large media organizations.

But there is something we have to remember, particularly in this country. While modern technology makes possible a much greater variety of forms of communication, there is another law of communication stated so well by Harold Innis a number of years ago: as means of communication become more sophisticated, there is an inevitable tendency toward concentration of ownership of those means. Economies of scale operate in most spheres of our economy, and particularly strongly in the field of communication. As the technology becomes more highly developed, the necessary capital investment becomes more expensive. As a result, daily newspapers have decreased in number, and those that remain tend to form into chains, leading to a remarkable concentration of ownership of newspapers in this country as in many other countries. The same trend toward group or common ownership can be seen in radio and television stations. Also, there has been a tendency for newspapers, where possible, to take over television stations, radio stations, and cable organizations and vice-versa.

Concentration works within the country, and also between countries. In Canada, there has been the real possibility of the ownership of newspapers, broadcasting stations, and other means of communication falling into non-Canadian hands. It has been found necessary to have laws and regulations deliberately aimed at preserving Canadian ownership, not just of broadcasting stations but also of daily newspapers and periodicals.

But it is not just concentration of ownership or means of distribution that should concern us; the control of the original creation of the message or the material to be transmitted is of great importance, and in this area the pressure toward concentration is particularly strong. As we all know, there are centres of production within countries: in Great Britain, production of all kinds tends to concentrate in London; in the United States, in Hollywood and New York; in Canada, for network broadcasting, in Toronto and Montreal.

This concentration occurs not just within countries; it takes place very much among countries. Canada has never been able to escape the enormous differentials in the costs of creative material for communication — the difference in cost, for use in Canada, between American and Canadian material. In Hollywood a half-hour of television that will attract viewers across the United States and also in Canada can be produced for, say, $50,000. The main cost is recovered in the huge American market, and the producer can make some additional money by making the program available for Canadian use for, perhaps, three or four or five thousand dollars. But to produce a program of the same entertainment quality in Canada would cost approximately the same amount as in Hollywood.

The history of films has shown the enormously strong productive power of Hollywood in spreading American films all over the world. This was an immense obstacle to the development of film making in most other countries, countered in some cases by deliberate national efforts to support and develop film production.

The same sort of thing tends to happen in the print media, although to a lesser extent. There have been lively discussions lately about Canadian periodicals that draw much of their material directly from some parent organization in the United States. It is also significant that our daily newspapers draw a major part of their feature material — for example, their comics, a highly read part of the paper, as well as many other regular features — from outside Canada.

Right through Canadian mass communication systems, there is enormous economic pressure for importing material and against producing our own. These factors provided one of the main reasons, probably the most important, for establishing the CBC in the first place. The CBC was to be supported by public funds so that it could and would, contrary to economic arithmetic, run east and west across the country, and produce and use a substantial proportion of Canadian material. This type of situation must be faced in all media, whatever the new technological developments. We must realize that in all fields of mass communication in Canada, it usually will be cheaper to import material, and more expensive to develop Canadian material. It will inevitably be necessary to continue, and probably to increase, public subsidies and other forms of public intervention to ensure that at least a reasonable part of the fare communicated by all these various means in Canada is of Canadian origin, that Canadians really are enabled to communicate among themselves by these means.

As mentioned, there is a tendency for production within a country to concentrate in one or two centres. At the same time, there seems to be an increasing desire for people to communicate within smaller groups, and some of the new technological developments make this far more possible either electronically, or by small newspapers produced by new and inexpensive methods. This will undoubtedly increase the development of media in Canada.

A most illustrative story concerns the arrival of the satellite and the establishment of ground stations in northern Canada. The CBC, it was assumed, would use these ground stations to pick up and rebroadcast material for a largely Eskimo population. The Inuit who came to hearings on the matter said, in effect: "You know, we aren't particularly interested in all this material from the United States and from southern Canada. What we want above all is to communicate among ourselves and with our outlying camps."

It is not only Eskimos, not only people in outlying areas, who are concerned. People in smaller communities right across Canada, even in communities within the coverage of other big media, seem to want more means of communication of their own; and they will now have increasing opportunities with modern technological developments.

In Canada there seems to be an increasing sense of regional identity, of regional concern, not just in Quebec but also in the Prairie provinces, British Columbia, the Maritimes, Northern Ontario, and other northern regions. On the whole, the development of our communication systems has not kept pace with the growth of those regional concerns and regional interests, and we are likely to see considerable development of more effective regional communication. A number of provincial governments would like more effective ways to communicate directly with their people, and of their people speaking among themselves. By the year 2000, we will surely see a much stronger regional component in our communication systems in Canada. Again, it must be pointed out that a high degree of public intervention and public action will be required, as regional development will not usually tend to be economically very rewarding.

We have started with technical possibilities and tried to guess what will happen; we should now raise the basic question of whether the nature of society is the result, or the cause, of its forms of communication; whether it is communication revolutions that make societies, or social conditions and demands that determine means of communicating.

Certainly, forms of communication have an enormous effect on how society develops. Yet the needs of people should ultimately determine how communication systems develop. We are all familiar with pessimistic thinkers of recent years who have kept saying that technology is leading us by the nose to a sad fate; that there is not much hope for the interesting and thoughtful kind of life. They rage at pressures against variety and individualism. It has been suggested by people such as George Orwell and Aldous Huxley that the effect of mass communication will be uniformity of thinking. I am suggesting that we seem to be going in the other direction, and that we can take an optimistic view.

I believe, in fact, the developments of technology are not only making possible but actually may be bringing about more specialization, more diversity in communication systems, more meeting of special concerns, and therefore a growing of particular diversified interests. I think it is very possible that increasingly the wealth of technological development may make it easier for us to be masters of technology, rather than its doltish subjects. In what is often referred to as post-industrial society, there is certainly going to be less concentration on production, and there is already more chance for leisure and for thought. We already have a public that not only is better educated in the formal way, but is more aware of all sorts of things going on in society and in the world about it. There is more demand for a variety of services and a variety of information, for the meeting of particular interests of people, in all sorts of subjects from physical fitness to welfare systems. I predict the development of the technological opportunities will feed the growth of the different interests in society. In short, I am optimistic. I believe that by the year 2000 we shall have in Canada a much more interesting communication system and, as a consequence, a more interesting society.

The large media organizations will have to calculate very carefully how to allocate their space and their efforts in trying to meet the increasingly specialized wants of various groups of people. I do not think daily newspapers are going to die. Although their death was prophesied by some people early in the electronic era, I am convinced that we shall continue to see things called daily newspapers twenty-five years from now. They may be produced by new processes, and may arrive in homes by some means quite different from the familiar carrier boy. However, I am sure there will be some means of having a great deal of current information available regularly in the home, in print form, for easy reference.

And a higher proportion of that material will be more thoughtful, more penetrating, less biased to the immediate and the titillating than at present, since there will be so many other means for the latter kind of news to be transmitted. There will be a trend — already noticeable in a number of the major newspapers in this country — toward less emphasis on spot news, on the quick story of a crime or a government statement or a quick reaction from somebody; and more on looking more deeply into what is happening in society, trying to spot trends. We can expect to see increasing efforts to develop the kinds of stories that are covered — not by a reporter going out for two or three hours and getting some fast reactions — but by weeks of research, observation, study, and trying to find out what really has happened in a corner of society or in a big institution.

All our major media should be doing more of this on a larger scale, and I hope local forms of communication will do more on the community scale. Already CBC radio is going quite a long way in this direction, and many thinking people are increasingly finding that it serves their interests and goes into things in a way that satisfies them more than television does.

This is an increasingly complex society. It is also a society in which big institutions play an increasingly large part. Large institutions, government and private, have a large effect on our daily lives, in a way that they didn't two or three generations ago. They affect everything all the time: how much money we make; what we do; the surroundings we live in; and so on. But as these institutions have grown, they have told us very little about their activities. The outward flow of information from them has not grown in any way proportionately to their growth. People have an increasing desire to see the big institutions of society become more answerable, more accountable, to society; to give us more chance to know what they are doing, and even to talk back to them occasionally.

The Ontario Press Council, of which I am Chairman, is a very interesting example of an attempt to make some big institutions — a group of daily newspapers, usually regarded as fiercely independent — a bit more answerable, more open, more accessible to members of the public. Its structure might be useful for other institutions or groups of institutions. The group of newspapers started by appointing myself as Chairman and picking ten professional people from different ranks of newspaper work to serve, not as representatives of their papers, but as knowledgeable professionals. The eleven of us then selected ten members of the public from different geographic, economic, and social backgrounds. This process produced a body of twenty-one people determined to be independent — some with high professional knowledge, others with a pretty good sense of what ordinary people think in different parts of the province.

The major function of the Council, but not its only one, is to receive and consider complaints from the public. If the newspaper concerned does not satisfy a complainant, the Council has a hearing on the matter, giving the paper and the complainant each a chance to have their say. Then the Council issues an adjudication. It does not have the power to punish or to fine, but its member papers are obligated to carry its adjudications when those adjudications affect them. We found this to be a pretty good sanction. I suggest we may be seeing more bodies like the Council in society, and that it will be very healthy if we do.

But we need more. Large institutions in general simply

are not doing enough to let people know what they are doing and thinking. A very big job for all the media within the next twenty-five years will be to pry into institutions to find out what they are doing; to dig out information; to do research on them; to help people to be able to make up their minds about institutions.

But not all the responsibility falls on the media. Much of it falls on the governments and other institutions themselves. Increasingly, they have become storehouses for immense supplies of information gathered at public expense with the support of taxpayers and consumers. A great deal of that information would be highly interesting to certain individuals and to certain groups among the public. If this information were more open, part of the job of the media would be to dig it out, select it, summarize it, and convey it, often by some specialized means, to people to whom it would be useful.

Under our kind of system of government there need to be exceptions to openness of information. One is Cabinet discussions and recommendations to Cabinet. I do not think there is need to reveal any given memo from one public servant to another, or confidential negotiations. In fact, I think now the media often spend a great deal of time trying to get at something that is not really very important — perhaps a whiff of a scandal — where they actually may be missing a whole area of bad administration, or not getting at a mine of information in some government office that could be extraordinarily valuable to members of the public.

I know from private conversations and from observation in Ottawa (I am sure the same is true at Queen's Park) that there are very able people, many of them young, working on whole series of analyses of situations, developing ideas for future action, meeting in committees and holding discussions, producing reports and surveys. Most of the resulting information never gets outside a department. I feel very strongly that governments in this country have an obligation to take major steps, not just to respond to prying members of parliaments or members of legislatures, but to make some of these masses of information and analyses readily available to the public through the media.

Incidentally, this does not apply only to public bodies; it also applies very much to big private organizations, to large corporations that also increasingly affect our lives all the time. One can see a trend: better financial information coming out to satisfy shareholders and people financially interested; corporations trying to explain a bit more about how they fit into society and serve the economy. Again, I think there should be a strong demand on large private organizations to make available much more information about what they are doing and about society and its environment.

In general, I think that by the year 2000 in Canada we shall probably have a pretty good overall communication system, more varied than it is now — providing we continue to watch certain things. First, we must watch very closely that there is not too much concentration of production in certain centres; we must take steps to see that people in different parts of the country can talk to each other and can talk among themselves. We must continue to take all the necessary steps, and they may be very large, to see that a substantial amount of communication material originates in Canada. We do not want to shut our windows to the world, by any means; but if communication is to have a meaning to Canada, we must take steps, and pay the cost, to produce enough so that Canadians may effectively communicate among themselves. We need to ensure that all these technical developments do lead to a reasonable balance between spheres of communication — international, national, regional, and local.

We can have a good system if the media take increasing

responsibility for looking at trends in society, examining the underlying things, going below the surface to ask questions about what people really think and feel. And with the media, the powers that be — the big institutions in society — share a very large responsibility for seeing that by the year 2000 Canadians are as well informed as the very effective means of communication of that time will make possible.

The Gerstein Lecturers

Pierre Juneau is Chairman of the National Capital Commission. He was born in Verdun, Quebec, and received his education at the Collège Sainte-Marie in Montreal and in Paris. He has served as Executive Director, Senior Assistant to the Commissioner, and Director of French-Language Productions for the National Film Board; Vice-Chairman of the Board of Broadcast Governors; and Chairman of the Canadian Radio-Television Commission.

Gordon B. Thompson is a systems engineer with Bell Northern Research, Ottawa, where he conducts research into the relationship between information technology and socio-economic systems. He was born in Kanata, Ontario, and educated at the University of Toronto. He is Vice President and Governor of the International Council on Computer Communication, and has published many articles and participated in numerous international conferences on communications and society.

H. Marshall McLuhan is Director of the Centre for Culture and Technology at the University of Toronto. Born in Edmonton, Alberta, he was educated at the University of Manitoba and Cambridge University, and has taught at St. Michael's College, University of Toronto, since 1946. Widely recognized for his original theories of the mass media, he is the author of *The Mechanical Bride, The Gutenberg Galaxy, Understanding Media,* and *The Medium Is the Massage.*

DAVIDSON DUNTON is Director of the Institute of Canadian Studies at Carleton University. Born in Montreal, he was educated at McGill University and in Europe. He was Chairman of the Canadian Broadcasting Corporation from 1945 to 1958, and President of Carleton University from 1958 to 1972. He has served as Chairman of the Council of Ontario Universities, President of the Association of Universities and Colleges of Canada, and Co-Chairman of the Royal Commission on Bilingualism and Biculturalism.